Learning and O to
Fast, Reliable tics and Lakehouses

*Angelica Lo Duca, Tim Meehan,
Vivek Bharathan, and Ying Su*

Beijing · Boston · Farnham · Sebastopol · Tokyo

Learning and Operating Presto

by Angelica Lo Duca, Tim Meehan, Vivek Bharathan, and Ying Su

Copyright © 2023 O'Reilly Media, Inc. All rights reserved.

Published by O'Reilly Media, Inc., 1005 Gravenstein Highway North, Sebastopol, CA 95472.

O'Reilly books may be purchased for educational, business, or sales promotional use. Online editions are also available for most titles (*https://oreilly.com*). For more information, contact our corporate/institutional sales department: 800-998-9938 or *corporate@oreilly.com*.

Acquisitions Editor: Aaron Black
Development Editor: Gary O'Brien
Production Editor: Ashley Stussy
Copyeditor: Sonia Saruba
Proofreader: Kim Wimpsett

Indexer: Ellen Troutman-Zaig
Interior Designer: David Futato
Cover Designer: Karen Montgomery
Illustrator: Kate Dullea

September 2023:   First Edition

Revision History for the First Edition

2023-09-19:   First Release

See *https://oreilly.com/catalog/errata.csp?isbn=9781098141851* for release details.

978-1-098-14185-1

[LSI]

Table of Contents

Preface

Data warehousing began by pulling data from operational databases into systems that were more optimized for analytics. These systems were expensive appliances to operate, which meant people were highly judicious about what data was ingested into their data warehousing appliance for analytics.

Over the years, demand for more data has exploded, far outpacing Moore's law and challenging legacy data warehousing appliances. While this trend is true for the industry at large, certain companies were earlier than others to encounter the scaling challenges this posed.

Facebook was among the earliest companies to attempt to solve this problem in 2012. At the time, Facebook was using Apache Hive to perform interactive analysis. As Facebook's datasets grew, Hive was found not to be as interactive (read: too slow) as desired. This is largely because the foundation of Hive is MapReduce, which, at the time, required intermediate datasets to be persisted to disk. This required a lot of I/O to disk for transient, intermediate result sets. So Facebook developed Presto, a new distributed SQL query engine designed as an in-memory engine without the need to persist intermediate result sets for a single query. This approach led to a query engine that processed the same query orders of magnitude faster, with many queries completing with less-than-a-second latency. End users such as engineers, product managers, and data analysts found they could interactively query fractions of large datasets to test hypotheses and create visualizations.

While Facebook was among the earliest companies, it was not alone in the problems it faced as datasets grew and outpaced hardware advances. The data lake architecture was developed to address these challenges by decoupling storage from compute and allowing storage to grow in cheaper distributed filesystems that utilized commodity hardware and, eventually, cloud storage systems. Concurrent with cheaper storage to store the ever-increasing data were compute systems to process the ever-increasing data. However, it wasn't immediately clear how users would interactively query data from the data lake—often, as with Facebook in 2012, users would attempt to use tools designed for offline purposes to transform data, which was incredibly slow.

It was in this setting that Presto was made open source in 2013 and quickly gained traction from other data pioneers, such as Airbnb, Uber, and Netflix. The problem faced at Facebook was far from unique—it was only encountered early. Over the years, the need to interactively query data quickly over distributed storage has only grown. As the usage has increased, so have the expectations from users: originally, interactive queries often suffered from inconsistent results, lack of schema evolution, and the inability to debug prior versions of tables. To match these expectations, table formats have evolved from the original Hive table format to offer richer features found in data warehousing appliances, such as ACID transaction support and indexes. Presto's architecture was designed to flexibly handle these needs, which brings us to the present-day architecture of the lakehouse: cheap distributed storage over a data lake, with performance that often matches that of warehousing appliances, and usability features that give much of the same functionality as the appliances, reducing the need to extract, transform, and load (ETL) the data into other systems.

Why We Wrote This Book

Deploying Presto to meet your team's warehouse and lakehouse infrastructure needs is not a minor undertaking. For the deployment to be successful, you need to understand the principles of Presto and the tools it provides. We wrote this book to help you get up to speed with Presto's basic principles so you can successfully deploy Presto at your company, taking advantage of one of the most powerful distributed query engines in the data analytics space today. The book also includes chapters on the ecosystem around Presto and how you can integrate other popular open source projects like Apache Pinot, Apache Hudi, and more to open up even more use cases with Presto. After reading this book, you should be confident and empowered to deploy Presto in your team, and feel confident maintaining it going forward.

Who This Book Is For

This book is for individuals who are building data platforms for their teams. Job titles may include data engineers and architects, platform engineers, cloud engineers, and/or software engineers. They are the ones building and providing the platform that supports a variety of interconnected products. Their responsibilities include making sure all the components can work together as a single, integrated whole; resolving data processing and analytics issues; performing data cleaning, management, transformation, and deduplication; and developing tools and technologies to improve the analytics platform.

Conventions Used in This Book

The following typographical conventions are used in this book:

Italic
> Indicates new terms, URLs, email addresses, filenames, and file extensions.

`Constant width`
> Used for program listings, as well as within paragraphs to refer to program elements such as variable or function names, databases, data types, environment variables, statements, and keywords.

`Constant width bold`
> Shows commands or other text that should be typed literally by the user.

`Constant width italic`
> Shows text that should be replaced with user-supplied values or by values determined by context.

 This element signifies a tip or suggestion.

 This element signifies a general note.

 This element indicates a warning or caution.

Using Code Examples

Supplemental material (code examples, exercises, etc.) is available for download at *https://github.com/alod83/Learning-and-Operating-Presto*.

If you have a technical question or a problem using the code examples, please send email to *bookquestions@oreilly.com*.

This book is here to help you get your job done. In general, if example code is offered with this book, you may use it in your programs and documentation. You do not need to contact us for permission unless you're reproducing a significant portion of the code. For example, writing a program that uses several chunks of code from this book does not require permission. Selling or distributing examples from O'Reilly books does require permission. Answering a question by citing this book and quoting example code does not require permission. Incorporating a significant amount of example code from this book into your product's documentation does require permission.

We appreciate, but generally do not require, attribution. An attribution usually includes the title, author, publisher, and ISBN. For example: *"Learning and Operating Presto* by Angelica Lo Duca, Tim Meehan, Vivek Bharathan, and Ying Su (O'Reilly). Copyright 2023 O'Reilly Media, Inc., 978-1-098-14185-1."

If you feel your use of code examples falls outside fair use or the permission given above, feel free to contact us at *permissions@oreilly.com*.

O'Reilly Online Learning

O'REILLY®   For more than 40 years, *O'Reilly Media* has provided technology and business training, knowledge, and insight to help companies succeed.

Our unique network of experts and innovators share their knowledge and expertise through books, articles, and our online learning platform. O'Reilly's online learning platform gives you on-demand access to live training courses, in-depth learning paths, interactive coding environments, and a vast collection of text and video from O'Reilly and 200+ other publishers. For more information, visit *https://oreilly.com*.

How to Contact Us

Please address comments and questions concerning this book to the publisher:

O'Reilly Media, Inc.
1005 Gravenstein Highway North
Sebastopol, CA 95472
800-889-8969 (in the United States or Canada)
707-829-7019 (international or local)
707-829-0104 (fax)
support@oreilly.com
https://www.oreilly.com/about/contact.html

We have a web page for this book, where we list errata, examples, and any additional information. You can access this page at *https://oreil.ly/learning-operating-presto-1e*.

For news and information about our books and courses, visit *https://oreilly.com*.

Find us on LinkedIn: *https://linkedin.com/company/oreilly-media*

Follow us on Twitter: *https://twitter.com/oreillymedia*

Watch us on YouTube: *https://youtube.com/oreillymedia*

Acknowledgments

This book results from the work of many collaborating people, each bringing their unique expertise, insights, and dedication to ensure its success. First, we would like to thank the technical reviewers, Chunxu Tang, Andreas Kaltenbrunner, and Scott Haines, who took the time to provide constructive feedback. Your insights and suggestions were crucial in shaping the final product, and we appreciate your dedication to helping improve the quality of this work.

Additionally, we sincerely thank Wen Phan for his generosity in sharing his expertise, especially in Chapter 5. Your knowledge and insights have greatly enriched the content, and we are truly grateful for your contributions.

We also would like to express our sincere gratitude to the acquisition editor at O'Reilly, Aaron Black, for believing in the concept of this book and allowing us to bring it to life. Your guidance and support throughout the process has been invaluable. To the development editor, Gary O'Brien, thank you for your unwavering commitment to making this book the best it can be. Your attention to detail and insightful suggestions have genuinely elevated the content, and we are grateful for your expertise and dedication.

Finally, a special thanks to the entire O'Reilly crew behind the scenes who worked tirelessly to ensure this book became a reality. Your hard work, professionalism, and enthusiasm are truly commendable.

Angelica Lo Duca

First, I thank my husband, Andrea, for his patience and encouragement in writing this book. Thanks for the words of comfort and our long chats about motivation. A warm thank you to my children, who, with their joy and games, have accompanied my hours spent typing on the computer, they with their books to write, and I with mine. Finally, a special thanks to the Lord and God of my life, Jesus Christ, for calling me to joyfully share the results of my studies and research. Because in everything, there is more joy in giving than in receiving.

Tim Meehan

To my wife and son, who were patient with me on this journey. To Girish Balliga for his insights and leadership of the Presto Foundation. To my colleagues at Meta and IBM for their friendship, support, guidance, and inspiration, in particular, James Sun, Masha Basmanova, Steven Mih, and Ali LeClerc.

Vivek Bharathan

Heartfelt thanks to my Presto community for conversations, edits, insights, and other contributions to this book. A special shout-out to Reetika Agrawal, Rohan Pednekar, and Devesh Agrawal. To Ali LeClerc, whose aid was invaluable in this collaboration. To Stephen Mih and Dipti Borkar, whose vision and inspiration brought us so far. To David Simmen's leadership and guidance. And finally, to my wife Priya and daughter Raksha whose steadfast support throughout this journey made it all possible.

Ying Su

To my dear parents, who gave me endless love, care, and support. Thanks Steven Mih, Dipti Borker, and David Simmen for their vision, courage, tireless work, and tremendous trust and support. Thanks to my colleagues at Ahana, IBM, and Meta for their friendship, guidance, and inspiration!

CHAPTER 1

Introduction to Presto

Over the last few years, the increasing availability of different data produced by users and machines has raised new challenges for organizations wanting to make sense of their data to make better decisions. Becoming a data-driven organization is crucial in finding insights, driving change, and paving the way to new opportunities. While it requires significant data, the benefits are worth the effort.

This large amount of data is available in different formats, provided by different data sources, and searchable with different query languages. In addition, when searching for valuable insights, users need results very quickly, thus requiring high-performance query engine systems. These challenges caused companies such as Facebook (now Meta), Airbnb, Uber, and Netflix to rethink how they manage data. They have progressively moved from the old paradigm based on data warehouses to data lakehouses. While a data warehouse manages structured and historical data, a data lakehouse can also manage and get insights from unstructured and real-time data.

Presto is a possible solution to the previous challenges. Presto is a distributed SQL query engine, created and used by Facebook at scale. You can easily integrate Presto in your data lake to build fast-running SQL queries that interact with data wherever your data is physically located, regardless of its original format.

This chapter will introduce you to the concept of the data lake and how it differs from the data warehouse. Then, you'll learn what Presto is, why it was created, and why it is used by so many companies. You'll also learn the most popular Presto use cases, such as ad hoc querying, reporting, and dashboarding. Finally, you'll become familiar with the case study you'll use throughout all the chapters.

Data Warehouses and Data Lakes

There are three main data types: *structured data*, *semi-structured data*, and *unstructured data*. Table 1-1 shows these data types, with a short description, the typical formats, the pros and cons, and some practical examples.

Table 1-1. Data types

	Structured data	Semi-structured data	Unstructured data
Description	Data is organized in a fixed schema	Data is partially organized without a fixed schema	Data is not organized
Typical formats	SQL, CSV	JSON, XML	Audio, video, text
Pros	Easy to derive insights	More flexible than structured data	Very scalable
Cons	Schema dependence limits scalability	The meta-level structure may contain unstructured data	Difficult to search
Examples	Database	Annotated texts, such as tweets with hashtag	Plain text, digital photos

Depending on the types of supported data and how they are organized and processed, there are different data storage systems. A *data warehouse* is a central repository containing *only* structured data and is used for reporting and analysis. Figure 1-1 shows the general architecture of a data warehouse. There are four main layers:

Structured data
> Includes structured data provided by multiple sources (e.g., relational database systems)

Extract, transform, and load (ETL)
> The process that converts data into a proper format

Data warehouse
> Contains data ready to be consumed by the final layers

Reporting, dashboarding, and data mining
> The final layers that consume data contained in the data warehouse

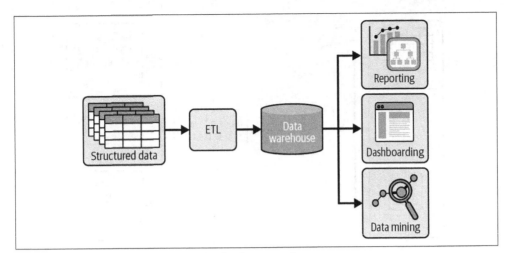

Figure 1-1. The general architecture of a data warehouse

With the advent of the big data era, the underlying architecture behind data warehouses has proven insufficient to manage large amounts of data. Big companies, such as Facebook, had the following issues with using data warehouses:

Unstructured data
Since a data warehouse manages structured data, it cannot be used to store raw unstructured data, such as text or audio. You must process unstructured data before ingesting it into a data warehouse.

Scalability
A data warehouse experiences a nonlinear increase in technical costs associated with the growing amounts of ingested data and analytical processing.

Real-time data
A data warehouse is not suitable for near-real-time data because data must be structured before it can be used.

A *data lake* addresses these issues. Figure 1-2 shows the general architecture of a data lake.

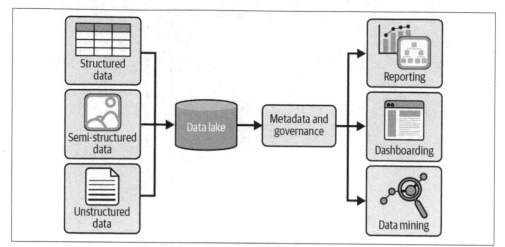

Figure 1-2. The general architecture of a data lake

Unlike a data warehouse, a data lake manages and provides ways to consume, or process, structured, semi-structured, and unstructured data. Ingesting raw data permits a data lake to ingest both historical and real-time data in a raw storage system. Over time, the concept of a data lake has evolved to the *data lakehouse*, an augmented data lake that includes support for transactions at its top. In practice, a data lakehouse modifies the existing data in the data lake, following the data warehouse semantics. We will discuss the concept of the data lakehouse and implement it in Chapter 5.

The early data lakes, called *on-premise data lakes*, were installed on company servers. The main advantage of this type of data lake was the total control of the system by the company. With the advent of cloud computing, data lakes have moved to the cloud, leaving the management, maintenance, and security issues to the cloud providers and their customers, who are both responsible for the security of their data. This is called a *cloud data lake*, and it is growing in popularity. The major platforms that provide cloud data lakes are Amazon Web Services (AWS), Azure, and Google Cloud via something called an *object store*.

To make data accessible to the upper layers (dashboarding, reporting, and data mining), a data lake provides an intermediate layer, called *metadata and governance*, which guarantees data consistency and security controls.

The Role of Presto in a Data Lake

Presto is an open source, distributed SQL query engine that supports structured and semi-structured data sources. You can use Presto to query your data directly where it is located, like a data lake, without the need to move the data to another system.

Presto runs queries concurrently through a memory-based architecture, making it very fast and scalable.

Within the data lake architecture, you can imagine that Presto fits into the governance and metadata layer. Presto executes queries directly in memory. Avoiding the need for writing and reading from disk between stages ultimately speeds up the query execution time.

The Presto coordinator machine analyzes any query written in SQL (supporting the ANSI SQL standard), creates and schedules a query plan on a cluster of Presto worker machines connected to the data lake, and then returns the query results. The query plan may have a number of execution stages, depending on the query. For example, if your query is joining many large tables, it may need multiple stages to execute, aggregating the tables. You can think of those intermediate results as your scratchpad for a long calculus problem.

Presto Origins and Design Considerations

Presto was implemented by Facebook in 2012 to overcome the issues derived from Apache Hive, a distributed SQL engine on top of the Hadoop MapReduce framework connected to its data lake. Apache Hive was one of Facebook's data warehouses used at the time. The main problem of Apache Hive included the fact that it was slow when dealing with huge quantities of data.

Apache Hive

Apache Hive was also originally developed and made open source by Facebook in 2010. At that time, the architecture underlying Apache Hive was MapReduce, which exploited intermediate datasets to be persisted to disk. This required frequent I/O access to the disk for data for transient, intermediate result sets.

To overcome these issues, Facebook developed Presto, a new distributed SQL query engine designed as an in-memory engine without the need to persist intermediate result sets for a single query. This approach led to a query engine that processed the same query faster by orders of magnitude with many queries completed with a latency of less than a second. End users, such as engineers, product managers, and data analysts, found they could interactively query subsets of large datasets to test hypotheses and create visualizations.

Figure 1-3 shows how Presto and Hive execute queries. Hive uses the MapReduce framework to run queries. In practice, it stores intermediate results to disk: both after the map and the reduce phases, the intermediate results are stored to the disk. Instead, Presto saves time by executing the queries in the memory of the worker machines, including performing operations on intermediate datasets there, instead of persisting them to disk.

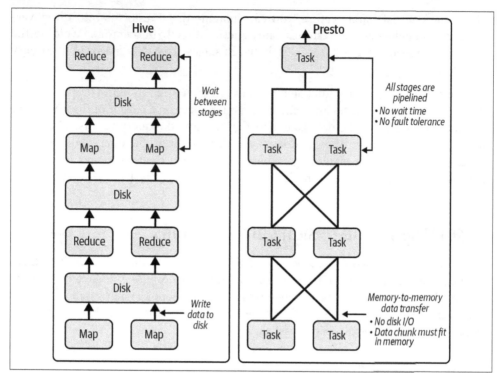

Figure 1-3. How Presto and Hive execute queries

In 2013, Facebook made the Presto GitHub repository open source under the Apache 2.0 license. Later, Facebook donated the project to be hosted by the Linux Foundation, which created a subfoundation called the Presto Foundation.

Presto was developed with the following design considerations: high performance, high scalability, compliance to the American National Standards Institute (ANSI) SQL standard, a federation of data sources, and the ability to run in the cloud.

High Performance

Presto defines several rules, including well-known optimizations such as predicate and limit pushdown, column pruning, and decorrelation. In practice, Presto can make intelligent choices on how much of the query processing can be pushed down into the data sources, depending on the source's abilities. For example, some data sources may be able to evaluate predicates, aggregations, function evaluation, etc. By pushing these operations closer to the data, Presto achieves significantly improved performance by minimizing disk I/O and network data transfer. The remainder of the query, such as joining data across different data sources, will be processed by Presto.

High Scalability

Thanks to its architecture that you'll see in the next section, Presto can run at any scale, although a large infrastructure isn't a requirement. You can also use Presto in small settings or for prototyping before tackling a larger dataset. Because of its very low latency, there isn't a major overhead for running small queries.

Compliance with the ANSI SQL Standard

Presto runs SQL queries, which adhere to the ANSI SQL standard. As most users already know how to write SQL queries, Presto is easily accessible and doesn't require learning a new language. Presto's SQL compliance immediately enables a large number of use cases.

What ANSI SQL Compliance Means

Being compliant with the ANSI SQL standard means that the major, commonly used commands, like SELECT, UPDATE, DELETE, INSERT, and JOIN, all operate as you'd expect.

Federation of Data Sources

A *federated query engine* is mapped to multiple data sources enabling unified access to those systems either for queries to a single data source at a time or for federated queries with multiple data sources.

Presto is a federated query engine that supports pluggable connectors to access data from and write data to external data sources—no matter where they reside. Many data sources are available for integration with Presto.

Federated Query Engine Versus Federated Query

The concept of a federated query engine is slightly different from that of the *federated query*. A federated query is a single query that stores or retrieves data from multiple different data sources, instead of a single data source. A *federated query engine* is a query engine specifically designed to execute federated queries. Presto is a federated query engine that supports federated queries.

Figure 1-4 illustrates the basic steps of how a query engine processes a federated query.[1] Upon receiving a query, the query engine parses it (*query parsing*) and accesses the sources catalog to select the data source or sources involved in the query (*data source selection*). As a result, source selection decomposes the query into subqueries.

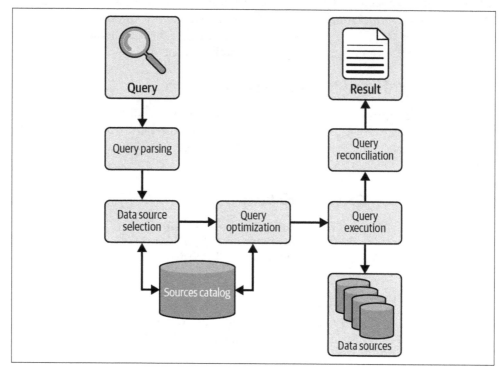

Figure 1-4. Basic steps of federated query processing

The next step involves building a logical plan (*query optimization*), which defines how the query is executed and which operators (JOIN, UNION, FILTER, and so on) should be used. An example of a logical plan is a *tree-based plan*, where the leaves of the tree correspond to the subqueries to be executed, and internal nodes represent the operators.

The logical plan is translated into a physical plan (*query execution*), which executes the query practically over the selected data sources. The outputs of the single subqueries are finally reconciled to build the final result (*query reconciliation*).

---

1 Kemele M. Endris, Maria-Esther Vidal, and Damien Graux, "Chapter 5, Federated Query Processing," in *Knowledge Graphs and Big Data Processing*, ed. Valentina Janev, Damien Graux, Hajira Jabeen, and Emanuel Sallinger (Springer, 2020), *https://oreil.ly/p7KFC*.

Running in the Cloud

You can run Presto in a cluster deployed by your company, or you can use an existing cloud service. There are many cloud offerings for running Presto, including Amazon Elastic MapReduce (EMR) and Google Dataproc. Other vendors, such as IBM, offer Presto as part of an open data lakehouse offering that makes it easier to set up and operate multiple Presto clusters for different use cases.

Presto Architecture and Core Components

Figure 1-5 shows the Presto architecture, which is deployed as two main services: a single coordinator and many workers. The coordinator service is effectively the brain of the operation, receiving query requests from clients, parsing the query, building an execution plan, and then scheduling work to be done across many worker services. The coordinator contains three main components: the parser, the planner, and the scheduler.

Each worker processes a part of the overall query in parallel, and you can add worker services to your Presto deployment to fit your demand. Each data source is configured as a catalog, and you can query as many catalogs as you want in each query.

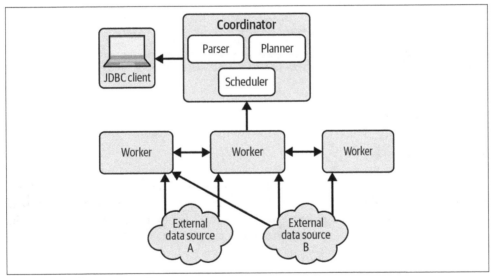

Figure 1-5. The Presto architecture

You can configure Presto in three different ways:

With only one data source
> Users can query a single data source with Presto. In this case, Presto becomes the separated query engine that uses the metadata from an external catalog and processes data stored in the data lake.

With multiple data sources queried independently
> As a federated engine, you can see many Presto deployments that are connected to multiple data sources. This allows end users to query one data source at a time, using the same interface without having to switch between systems or think of them as different data systems.

With multiple data sources, correlated and queried together
> Taking federation a step further, a query can combine data from two or more data sources. The benefits of doing so allow end users to analyze more data without the need to move or copy data into a single data source.

Table 1-2 outlines the benefits provided by the different configurations. Single sources only provide fast analytics. Presto configured with multiple data sources, each queried independently, gives you fast, federated analytics. Finally, if Presto is configured with multiple data sources, correlated and queried together, it gives you fast, federated, unified analytics.

Table 1-2. Benefits provided by the different configurations of Presto

Type of source	Fast analytics	Federated analytics	Unified analytics
Single source	X	-	-
Multiple sources queried independently	X	X	-
Multiple sources queried together	X	X	X

Alternatives to Presto

Many alternatives to Presto have been proposed by the research community. Research has focused on building a fast and scalable, distributed query engine, able to deal with big data. Given the constant growth of big data, solutions like Presto and its alternatives have become very attractive to the industry.

Apache Impala

Apache Impala, originally developed by Cloudera, is a distributed SQL query engine for Apache Hadoop. You can use Apache Impala for medium-sized datasets, although it does not support some SQL operations, such as UPDATE and DELETE. Apache Impala is supported by Amazon Web Services and MapR.

Apache Hive

Apache Hive is data warehouse software for managing large datasets queried using the SQL syntax. Built on Apache Hadoop, Hive supports different data formats, such as comma- and tab-separated values (CSV/TSV) text files, Apache Parquet, and more. You can extend Hive with a custom connector to support other data formats. You can also use Hive with Presto.

Spark SQL

Spark SQL is a module built for Apache Spark to work with structured data. You can also use it as a distributed SQL query engine, and you can integrate it with the rest of the Spark modules.

Spark Versus Presto

Spark and Presto manage stages differently. In Spark, data needs to be fully processed before passing it to the next stage. Presto uses a pipeline processing approach and doesn't need to wait for an entire stage to finish.

Trino

When the founders of the Presto project left Facebook in 2018, the original project, PrestoDB (described in this book), was forked into a separate project, called PrestoSQL. In 2021, PrestoSQL was rebranded as Trino.

Similar to Presto, Trino aims at running fast and federated queries, without copying and moving data from sources to temporary storage.

Presto Use Cases

Presto was originally designed for interactive analytics and ad hoc querying. With the evolution of technology and the availability of near-real-time data, the number of use cases where Presto is applied has increased. In this section, you'll see the most popular use cases for Presto.

Reporting and Dashboarding

Unlike the first-generation static versions, today's interactive reporting and dashboards are very different. Analysts, data scientists, product managers, marketers, and other users not only want to look at Key Performance Indicators (KPIs), product statistics, telemetry data, and other data, but they also want to drill down into specific areas of interest or areas where opportunity may lie.

Presto gives users the ability to query data across sources on their own so they're not dependent on data platform engineers. It also greatly simplifies data platform engineer tasks by providing them with a single endpoint for many reporting and dashboarding tools, including Tableau, Graphana, Apache Superset, and much more.

Ad Hoc Querying

Engineers, analysts, data scientists, and product managers can customize their queries either manually or using a range of visualization, dashboarding, and Business Intelligence (BI) tools. Depending on the tools chosen, they can run many complex concurrent queries against a Presto cluster. With Presto, they can iterate quickly on innovative hypotheses with the interactive exploration of any dataset, residing anywhere.

ETL Using SQL

Analysts can aggregate terabytes of data across multiple data sources and run efficient ETL (extract, transform, and load) queries against that data with Presto. Instead of legacy batch processing systems, you can use Presto to run resource-efficient and high-throughput queries.

Running queries in batch ETL jobs is much more expensive in terms of data volume and CPU than running interactive jobs. Because the clusters tend to be much bigger, some companies separate Presto clusters into two groups: one for ETL and the other for ad hoc queries. This is operationally advantageous because the two clusters use the same Presto technology and require the same skills.

ETL Versus ELT

ETL (extract, transform, and load) differs from ELT (extract, load, and transform), although the performed operations are the same in both processes. The difference is not simply the order of the operations, because usually they are performed in parallel. Instead, the difference is *where* the transformation of data is performed. In an ETL system, transformation is performed in a staging area of the data warehouse, while in an ELT system, transformation is performed directly in the backend data warehouse.

Data Lakehouse

A data lake enables you to store all your structured and unstructured data as is and run different types of analytics on it. A data lakehouse has SQL workloads and also other non-SQL workloads (e.g., machine learning on unstructured data). Presto handles the SQL workloads. You can use Presto to run SQL queries directly on your data lake without moving them or transforming them.

Real-Time Analytics with Real-Time Databases

Real-time analytics usually involves combining data that is being captured in real time with historical or archived data. Imagine that an ecommerce site uses two stores: the first store is, for example, an Amazon S3 bucket that stores your past activity, and the second is an Apache Pinot real-time store that stores your real-time activity, such as the content of your cart.

Also, imagine that your current session activity is moved from the real-time store to the historical archive at regular intervals. At a given instant, your current session activity may not make it into S3. By using Presto to merge data across both systems, the website could provide you with real-time incentives so you don't abandon your cart, or it could determine if there's possible fraud happening earlier and with greater accuracy.

Introducing Our Case Study

You can use Presto in different scenarios, including data-mining analytics, high-performance business intelligence analytics, and real-time monitoring. To show Presto's capabilities, we have built a fictional scenario that we'll use throughout the book, whenever possible.

Imagine that an ecommerce company offers a service that sells or distributes some products worldwide, such as books, clothes, and other items. To represent the service, we will use the Transaction Processing Performance Council Benchmark H (TPC-H) database, which is fully compatible with Presto.

The TPC-H database (*https://oreil.ly/rg6CG*) defines eight tables, as illustrated in Figure 1-6. The arrows in the figure show the relationships among the tables. The TPC-H database defines a generic ecommerce scenario that you can use for testing purposes, with a variable amount of data.

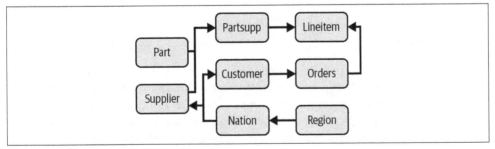

Figure 1-6. The TPC-H database

Figure 1-7 shows the architecture of our case study. There are two main data sources:

Real-time customer activity
    Defines the real-time events generated by the customer, such as the products in the cart

Products database
    Contains the products catalog

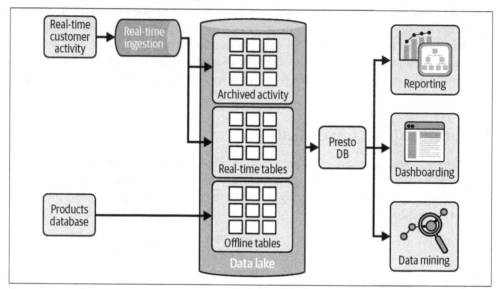

Figure 1-7. The architecture of our case study

Both data sources are ingested in the data lake. Periodically, the real-time customer activity is moved to a specific segment of the data lake, called *archived activity*. Presto accesses the data lake to perform different types of queries. At the top layers are the reporting, dashboarding, and data mining services.

Conclusion

In this chapter, you learned what Presto is and its role in a data lake. Presto is a parallel distributed SQL query engine for querying any data format: structured, semi-structured, or unstructured. You can use Presto to run queries in the context of big data, using ANSI SQL, a single standard and well-known language. You can also use Presto in scenarios requiring high performance and high scalability, and running in the cloud.

You now know the basic concepts behind Presto, including its architecture, how it runs federated queries, and its use cases. You now should be able to move a step further by installing and running your first scenario using Presto.

In Chapter 2, you will learn how to start with Presto, focusing on how to install and configure Presto using Docker and Kubernetes.

Getting Started with Presto

There are various ways to set up Presto. In the first part of this chapter, you'll see how to install Presto manually. We won't dwell much on manual installation, because the real goal of the chapter is to build a small cluster locally, which simulates a realistic production environment.

Next, you'll see how to install Presto on Docker and how to set up a local cluster in Kubernetes. Finally, you'll learn how to run your first queries in Presto, with a focus on how to list catalogs and schemas, and query a table.

This chapter assumes that you have some familiarity with Docker, Kubernetes, and using a command line. Even if you don't, you should still be able to follow the instructions end to end and get a working deployment running successfully.

Presto Manual Installation

To set up Presto on your local machine, you can follow the procedure described in the Presto official documentation (*https://oreil.ly/mqIXQ*). Since Presto is written in Java, you should pay attention to the specific versions of Java supported by Presto. Presto requires Java 8. Both Oracle JDK and OpenJDK are supported.

Running Presto on Docker

The local Presto instance is great for development and troubleshooting. You can set up a full production cluster with multiple nodes using bare-metal machines or VMs. However, you would need to manage the monitoring, availability, scalability, and rollout of these nodes by yourself. This is where containers and Kubernetes come in.

In this section, we'll install and run Presto on Docker, and in the next section, we'll set up an almost production-ready cluster using the same container binaries and a Kubernetes deployment configuration of a full-fledged cluster.

Running Presto on Docker is useful when running Presto as a standalone node, not connected to other external components, such as Apache Ranger for access control. Instead, if you require a more complex network, you must configure a more complex scenario, for example, based on Kubernetes. In this book, we'll use the Presto Docker as a basic container, and Kubernetes to set up a network of containers.

Installing Docker

You need to have a version of Docker installed to run a container. We have tested the code described in this book with Docker 4.2.0, but the most recent versions should work also. Docker requires at least 4 GB of RAM. However, we recommend at least 8 GB of RAM to improve Presto's performance. You can use either Docker Desktop (*https://oreil.ly/2DeFt*) on Windows or Mac, or Docker Engine (*https://oreil.ly/MZaWy*) on Linux. Make sure you are logged in via `docker login` to the Docker registry or another registry such as ECR to be able to publish your created images for use.

Presto Docker Image

Start by cloning the repository if you haven't already cloned it:

```
git clone https://github.com/alod83/Learning-and-Operating-Presto.git
```

The code used in this section is available in the directory *02/presto-docker*, which contains the following files, along with the *README.md* file:

Dockerfile
> The configuration file for Docker

etc/
> The directory containing the configuration files for Presto

In the remainder of this section, we'll describe the *Dockerfile* and the content of the *etc/* directory, which will allow you to customize your Presto installation. If you want to install Presto with the default configuration, you can skip ahead to "Building and Running Presto on Docker" on page 23.

Dockerfile

The *Dockerfile*, which is based on CentOS 7, installs the Presto server and the Presto client, along with other dependencies and tools. The *Dockerfile* is organized as follows.

First, define the basic image; the arguments, which include the Presto version to download; and the URLs to the Presto server and client binary files:

```
FROM centos:7
ARG PRESTO_VERSION
ARG PRESTO_BIN=https://repo1.maven.org/maven2/com/\
   facebook/presto/presto-server/${PRESTO_VERSION}/\
   presto-server-${PRESTO_VERSION}.tar.gz
ARG PRESTO_CLI_BIN=https://repo1.maven.org/maven2/com/\
   facebook/presto/presto-cli/${PRESTO_VERSION}/\
   presto-cli-${PRESTO_VERSION}-executable.jar
```

Installing Centos on ARM-Based Architectures

If your local machine has an ARM-based architecture (such as the modern Apple notebooks), the Docker build process may fail. You could solve the problem by importing amd64/centos:7 as the base image for your *Dockerfile* and then running the Docker container with the --platform linux/amd64 option, as described later in this section.

Next, install the required software to install Presto:

```
RUN yum update -y &&\
    yum install -y wget ca-certificates tar less\
    yum install -y java-1.8.0-openjdk\
    yum clean all
```

Create the */opt* directory, where you'll install Presto. Then, download the Presto server and client binaries and move them to the */opt* directory:

```
RUN mkdir -p /opt
RUN wget --quiet ${PRESTO_BIN}
RUN tar -xf presto-server-${PRESTO_VERSION}.tar.gz -C /opt
RUN rm presto-server-${PRESTO_VERSION}.tar.gz
RUN ln -s /opt/presto-server-${PRESTO_VERSION} /opt/presto
RUN wget --quiet "${PRESTO_CLI_BIN}"
RUN mv presto-cli-${PRESTO_VERSION}-executable.jar /usr/local/bin/presto
RUN chmod +x /usr/local/bin/presto
RUN mkdir /opt/presto/data
RUN mkdir /opt/presto/log
```

Now, copy the content of the *etc/* directory in your local filesystem to the *etc/* directory in the Docker image:

```
COPY etc /opt/presto/etc
```

Mounting the Local Filesystem in the Docker Container

Using the `COPY etc /opt/presto/etc` statement in the *Dockerfile* requires rebuilding the Docker image whenever you want to add something to your configuration. A possible alternative could be removing the previous statement and mounting a directory of your local filesystem in the Docker container. You can do it at runtime by specifying `-v <source_path>:<dest_path>` when you run the Docker container, as specified next in this section.

Finally, specify the command to run Presto:

```
CMD ["/opt/presto/bin/launcher", "run"]
```

The etc/ directory

The *etc/* directory contains the Presto configuration files. In this section, we'll see how to set up a basic configuration that runs Presto locally. The scenario uses a coordinator and just one worker. In "Building and Running Presto on Docker" on page 23, you'll learn how to configure Presto for a production-like environment. For now, the described configuration is sufficient to get started and get familiar with Presto.

The *etc/* directory contains the following basic files and directories:

- *node.properties*
- *jvm.config*
- *config.properties*
- *log.properties*
- *catalog/*

You can use the configuration files as described or try to modify them to customize the Presto configuration based on your needs. We'll analyze the configuration files in detail in subsequent chapters of the book.

node.properties.   A node is an instance of Presto, and this file is a configuration specific to the node. The following code snippet shows the minimum properties you must define in *node.properties*:

```
node.environment=presto_local
node.id=1a674699-500c-414c-b480-9ac0df416403
node.data-dir=data
```

The minimum required properties include:

node.environment
> This configuration specifies the name of the environment. All nodes in a Presto cluster must have the same environment name.

node.id
> A unique identifier for this installation of Presto. All the nodes in the same Presto installation must share the same node.id value, which must remain consistent across reboots and upgrades. You can generate this ID as a Universally Unique Identifier (UUID).

node.data-dir
> This configuration specifies the data directory where Presto will store logs and other data.

jvm.config. Presto is written in Java, so you can use this configuration file to store the command-line options that are passed to the Java Virtual Machine (JVM). To get started with Presto, we'll use the following options:

```
-server
-Xms3G
-Xmx3G
-Djdk.attach.allowAttachSelf=true
```

The -server option selects the Java HotSpot Server VM. The -Xms3G -Xmx3G option preallocates 3 GB of memory (min and max set to the same value) for the JVM. The -Djdk.attach.allowAttachSelf=true option is required to avoid startup errors by allowing the process to attach to the JVM to obtain information from instrumented objects.

We will cover this configuration file in more detail in Chapter 6.

config.properties. Use this file to specify the configuration of the Presto server. A node can be configured as a coordinator, a worker, or both. We will use the following configuration of our local Presto deployment of the Presto coordinator:

```
coordinator=true
node-scheduler.include-coordinator=true
http-server.http.port=8080
memory.heap-headroom-per-node=0.5GB
query.max-memory=1GB
query.max-memory-per-node=0.5GB
query.max-total-memory-per-node=2GB
discovery-server.enabled=true
discovery.uri=http://localhost:8080
```

Here is the explanation of the properties:

coordinator
> Specifying the value as `true` will allow this Presto node to accept client requests and manage the client connection.

node-scheduler.include-coordinator
> Specifying the value as `true` will allow scheduling work on the coordinator. You typically don't want this set as true in production because coordination and query execution will compete for the same resources. We'll discuss details about scheduling in Chapter 3.

http-server.http.port
> This is the HTTP port to use for communication among nodes and externally.

query.max-memory
> This is the maximum amount of user memory that a query can exploit across the Presto cluster. If a query exceeds this memory limit, Presto kills its execution automatically.

query.max-memory-per-node
> This is the maximum amount of user memory that a query can use on a worker. If a query exceeds this memory limit on any node, Presto kills its execution automatically.

query.max-total-memory-per-node
> This is the maximum amount of the sum of user and system memory that a query can use on a worker. If a query exceeds this memory limit on any node, Presto kills its execution automatically. We'll see the concepts of system and user memory in Chapter 6.

discovery-server.enabled
> All the nodes in the Presto cluster will automatically register with a *discovery service* when they start. To avoid running an additional service, the Presto coordinator can run an embedded version of the discovery service. This will allow you to set a single port for all your Presto machines and make deployment simpler.

discovery.uri
> This is the URI to the discovery server. Because we have enabled the embedded version of discovery in the Presto coordinator, this should be the URI of the Presto coordinator. The URI must match the host and port of the Presto coordinator. This URI must not end in a slash.

log.properties. Logging is essential to understand what the server is doing and troubleshoot issues. There are four levels: DEBUG, INFO, WARN, and ERROR. You can specify additional packages at the appropriate log level as needed. To get started, you can use the following configuration:

```
com.facebook.presto=INFO
```

By setting the `com.facebook.presto` package to `INFO`, you can see all the settings for the node at startup as well as any relevant information required for troubleshooting. We'll cover more of these settings in Chapter 6.

catalog/<connector>.properties. This directory contains the configuration for each connector used by your Presto configuration. As briefly introduced in Chapter 1, Presto uses connectors to access data from disparate data sources. Connectors are what make the *SQL on Anything* paradigm possible for the end users. Presto uses the native interfaces for the data sources to query and process data; for example, for relational databases, the connectors will use JDBC to access the data from the source, while for nonrelational sources such as S3, Elastic, etc., the connector will use the appropriate SDK/API.

As such, the connector could be interacting with the underlying data source using SQL, RESTful API, HTTP, or any other proprietary communication mechanism—all of this occurs behind the scenes. The connector abstracts the underlying data access for you into database, schema, table, and SQL constructs even if the underlying source has no concept of databases, schemas, or tables. As a user querying data via Presto, all you need to know is how to write an SQL query; the connector takes care of the rest. We'll discuss connectors in more detail in Chapter 3.

A connector establishes a connection between Presto and a catalog. You query a catalog using SQL. The connector abstracts the underlying complexity of interacting with the data source—it doesn't matter if it's a flat file, a NoSQL database, an API, or an RDBMS.

You register a catalog by creating a catalog properties file in the *etc/catalog* directory. For example, to mount the TPC-H catalog, you can create a `tpch.properties` with the following contents to mount the `tpch` connector as the `tpch` catalog:

```
connector.name=tpch
```

Building and Running Presto on Docker

Now you are ready to build your Docker image by running the following command in your terminal:

```
docker build --build-arg PRESTO_VERSION=0.276.1 . -t prestodb:latest
```

You need to pass the PRESTO_VERSION you want to install as an argument in the Docker command. At the time of writing, the last version of Presto is 0.276.1.

Then, you run the built image:

```
docker run --name presto prestodb:latest
```

The Presto server starts. You should see many logs and information in the standard input and standard error. You will know that the server is running if, after these logs and information, you see the following message:

```
INFO    main    com.facebook.presto.server.PrestoServer
======== SERVER STARTED ========
```

To test if the Presto server is running correctly, you can open a new terminal and connect to the Presto client within your Docker container:

```
docker exec -it presto presto
```

Now you are connected to your Presto client, and you can run a query, for example, showing the list of catalogs:

```
presto> show catalogs;
```

The query produces the following output:

```
Catalog
-------
 system
 tpch
(2 rows)

Query 20220919_085038_00001_j5vrm, FINISHED, 1 node
Splits: 19 total, 19 done (100.00%)
0:22 [0 rows, 0B] [0 rows/s, 0B/s]
```

The output of the query shows that there are two catalogs, system and tpch. This demonstrates that Presto has loaded the tpch catalog correctly.

The Presto Sandbox

So far, we have described how to build a basic Presto Docker container from scratch. If you need to install more packages or libraries for your scenario, you can use the Docker Presto sandbox container (*https://oreil.ly/PPmtr*). The Presto sandbox is already equipped with all the libraries required to configure many scenarios, such as a data lakehouse, as we'll see in Chapter 5. To run a Presto container using the Presto sandbox, follow the documentation (*https://oreil.ly/h6_xK*).

Deploying Presto on Kubernetes

Figure 2-1 shows the cluster we're going to deploy in our local machine. We'll use two data sources, TPC-H and a MySQL database. We'll deploy a single coordinator and two workers, each representing a pod in Kubernetes. This scenario requires at least 4 GB of RAM for each node, so if your machine doesn't have enough memory or storage capabilities, you could reduce the number of workers to one. You could create a new pod with a Presto client, but that is resource intensive. In this chapter, to reduce the number of resources used on the local computer, we'll use the Presto client available in the coordinator.

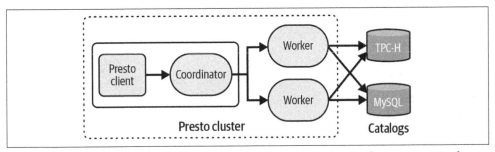

Figure 2-1. The scenario deployed in Kubernetes with a single coordinator, two workers, and two catalogs

Introducing Kubernetes

To build the local cluster we'll use throughout this chapter, you need to have Kubernetes installed locally on your computer. There are various flavors of Kubernetes out there; which flavor of Kubernetes you use doesn't matter. All interactions with Kubernetes are via kubectl, so make sure you have the Kubernetes client installed. You can find the instructions for your OS here (*https://oreil.ly/7yuDg*).

In this book, we'll use the version of Kubernetes provided by Docker Desktop. To install it, first you must install Docker Desktop, as described in the previous section, and then you can enable Kubernetes as follows:

1. Launch Docker Desktop and access the Dashboard.
2. Click the Settings button, located in the top-right part of the window.
3. From the left sidebar menu, select Kubernetes, then select "Enable Kubernetes," and finally click the "Apply & Restart" button.

Configuring Presto on Kubernetes

The code used in this section is available in the directory *02/presto-kubernetes* in the book's GitHub repository, which contains the following files, along with the *README.md* file:

presto-coordinator.yaml
> The configuration file for the Presto coordinator

presto-workers.yaml
> The configuration file for a Presto worker

presto-config-map.yaml
> Used to configure Presto dynamically

presto-secrets.yaml
> Used to store secrets in Presto

MySQL configuration files
> Used to add a MySQL catalog

deploy.sh
> A script used to deploy the cluster

Figure 2-2 shows how the *.yaml* files used to configure the coordinator and the workers are related each other.

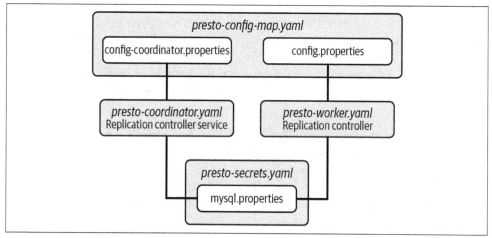

Figure 2-2. The relation among the .yaml files for the coordinator and the workers

In the remainder of this section, we'll describe the *.yaml* files, which will allow you to customize your Presto Kubernetes cluster, and in "Adding a New Catalog" on page 31, we'll show how to add a MySQL catalog and the *deploy.sh* script. If you want to run the Presto cluster with the default configuration, you can jump ahead to the next section.

presto-coordinator.yaml

This configuration file deploys the Presto coordinator as a replication controller and builds the associated service. First, build the service and name it presto-coordinator:

```
apiVersion: v1
kind: Service
metadata:
  name: presto-coordinator
spec:
  ports:
    - port: 8080
      protocol: TCP
      targetPort: 8080
  type: LoadBalancer
  selector:
    app: presto-coordinator
```

Then, build the replication controller, and use the local Docker image built in the previous section:

```
---
apiVersion: v1
kind: ReplicationController
metadata:
  name: presto-coordinator
spec:
  replicas: 1
  template:
    metadata:
      labels:
        app: presto-coordinator
    spec:
      containers:
        - name: presto-coordinator
          image: prestodb:latest
          imagePullPolicy: Never
          ports:
            - containerPort: 8080
            - containerPort: 8889
          resources:
            requests:
              memory: "4Gi"
            limits:
              memory: "4Gi"
```

Managing the Memory of Your Local Computer

When you configure the memory to assign to your pod, you should pay attention to the maximum memory available in your local machine. In fact, the sum of the memory allocated to all the pods must not exceed the total memory of your computer. If this happens, Kubernetes won't be able to allocate some pods in your cluster.

If you want to pull the image from a Docker registry, you need to push it to the registry in advance.

When we built the Docker image, we deployed the Presto controller and the worker on the same machine. Now we separate them, so we need to customize the *config.properties* configuration file to specify if the node is the controller of a worker. There are different ways to change this configuration. The simplest involves changing the configuration file within the Docker image. However, this solution requires rebuilding the Docker image. In this chapter, we use *ConfigMap* and *Secret* to solve this problem.

A ConfigMap stores nonconfidential data in key–value pairs. A Kubernetes pod can consume a ConfigMap as command-line arguments, as environment variables, or as configuration files mounted in a volume. In our scenario, the coordinator and the workers use the ConfigMap to store the Presto configuration files. A Secret stores sensitive information in key–value pairs. In our scenario, the coordinator and the workers use the Secret to store information related to the MySQL catalog.

The coordinator mounts the *config.properties* file specified in the ConfigMap and the *mysql.properties* file specified in the Secret as follows:

```
volumeMounts:
  - name: config
    mountPath: "/opt/presto/etc/config.properties"
    subPath: config.properties
  - name: mysql
    mountPath: "/opt/presto/etc/catalog/mysql.properties"
    subPath: mysql.properties
```

Now, we specify the volumes to mount. We'll use two volumes, a ConfigMap, for non-sensitive information, and a Secret, for sensitive information. We'll see the structure of the ConfigMap and the Secret later in this section. For now, you should focus only on how to configure them for the Presto coordinator. Configure the ConfigMap and the Secret as follows:

```
volumes:
    - name: config
      configMap:
        name: presto-config
        - key: "config-coordinator.properties"
```

```
        path: "config.properties"
    - name: mysql
        secret:
          secretName: presto-mysql-secrets
```

For the ConfigMap, you are specifying that the *config-coordinator.properties* file in the ConfigMap is saved to the file *config.properties* in the pod.

Then, mount the related volumes:

```
volumeMounts:
  - name: config
    mountPath: "/opt/presto/etc/config.properties"
    subPath: config.properties

  - name: mysql
    mountPath: "/opt/presto/etc/catalog/mysql.properties"
    subPath: mysql.properties
```

You are mapping the content of the `config` volume declared previously to the *config.properties* file in the pod, and the `mysql` volume declared previously to the *mysql.properties* file in the pod.

presto-workers.yaml

This configuration file deploys one or many Presto workers as replication controllers. The configuration file for the workers is quite similar to that of the coordinator because we use the same Docker image to build it:

```
---
apiVersion: v1
kind: ReplicationController
metadata:
  name: presto-worker
spec:
  replicas: 2
  template:
    metadata:
      labels:
        app: presto-worker
    spec:
      containers:
        - name: presto-worker
          image: prestodb:latest
          imagePullPolicy: Never
          resources:
            requests:
              memory: "4Gi"
            limits:
              memory: "4Gi"
          ports:
            - containerPort: 8080
```

You can change the number of workers by changing the value corresponding to the keyword `replicas`. In our case, we'll create two workers.

Similar to the coordinator configuration file, in the worker configuration file, we configure the Secret and the ConfigMap, except for using a different *config.properties*:

```
volumeMounts:
    - name: config
      mountPath: "/opt/presto/etc/config.properties"
      subPath: config.properties
    - name: mysql
        mountPath: "/opt/presto/etc/catalog/mysql.properties"
        subPath: mysql.properties

volumes:
    - name: config
      configMap:
        name: presto-config
        - key: "config.properties"
          path: "config.properties"
    - name: mysql
      secret:
        secretName: presto-mysql-secrets
```

presto-config-map.yaml

We use this file to store the configuration to pass to the coordinator and workers pods. You can customize this file if you want to add a new configuration for Presto. In our case, we specify two different versions of the *config.properties* file, one for the workers, and the other for the coordinator:

```
apiVersion: v1
kind: ConfigMap
metadata:
  name: presto-config
data:
  config.properties: |
    coordinator=false
    http-server.http.port=8080
    memory.heap-headroom-per-node=0.5GB
    query.max-memory=1GB
    query.max-memory-per-node=0.5GB
    query.max-total-memory-per-node=2GB
    discovery.uri=http://presto-coordinator:8080
  config-coordinator.properties: |
    coordinator=true
    node-scheduler.include-coordinator=true
    http-server.http.port=8080
    memory.heap-headroom-per-node=0.5GB
    query.max-memory=1GB
    query.max-memory-per-node=0.5GB
    query.max-total-memory-per-node=2GB
```

```
discovery-server.enabled=true
discovery.uri=http://presto-coordinator:8080
```

The two configurations are quite similar, except for three parameters: `coordinator`, `discovery-server.enabled`, and `node-scheduler.include-coordinator`.

presto-secrets.yaml

To store the configuration of the MySQL catalog, we use a Kubernetes Secret. You can customize this file if you want to add a new catalog for Presto. In our case, we specify the details for the MySQL catalog, as shown in the following code:

```
---
apiVersion: v1
stringData:
  mysql.properties: |-
    connector.name=mysql
    connection-url=jdbc:mysql://mysql:3306
    connection-user=root
    connection-password=dbuser
kind: Secret
metadata:
  name: presto-mysql-secrets
type: Opaque
```

To connect a MySQL catalog to Presto, we must specify the `connector.name`, the MySQL `connection-url`, and the MySQL credentials (`connection-user` and `connection-password`).

Adding a New Catalog

To create a new catalog, you must define both the deployment and the service providing the interface for the Presto connector. In this chapter, we'll describe how to build a MySQL catalog, but you can adapt the procedure for any catalog.

You can find the configuration of the MySQL catalog in the following files in the book's GitHub repository:

mysql-pv.yaml
Creates the persistent volume used as storage for the MySQL database.

mysql-deployment.yaml
Creates both the deployment and service for the MySQL server. The deployment reads the configuration parameters, such as the password, from the secrets stored in the *mysql-secrets.yaml* configuration file.

mysql-secrets.yaml

> Generates the secrets for the MySQL server. Secrets are encrypted using base64 encoding. To generate a secret, you can run the following command in a terminal: `echo -n "my_password" | base64`.

Running the Deployment on Kubernetes

To run the deployment, run the `deploy.sh` script:

```
./deploy.sh -d
```

You can also use the `-r` option to delete the cluster, and the `-b` option to first remove and then deploy the cluster.

Alternatively, you can deploy the cluster as follows:

1. Create a namespace for your cluster:

   ```
   kubectl create namespace presto
   ```

2. Create the MySQL deployment:

   ```
   kubectl create -f mysql-secrets.yaml --namespace presto
   kubectl apply -f mysql-pv.yaml --namespace presto
   kubectl apply -f mysql-deployment.yaml --namespace presto
   ```

3. Deploy the Presto Secret and the ConfigMap:

   ```
   kubectl create -f presto-secrets.yaml --namespace presto
   kubectl apply -f presto-config-map.yaml --namespace presto
   ```

4. Deploy the coordinator and the workers:

   ```
   kubectl apply -f presto-coordinator.yaml --namespace presto
   kubectl apply -f presto-workers.yaml --namespace presto
   ```

Your cluster is now active. You can check the status of each pod in the cluster as follows:

```
kubectl get pods --namespace presto
```

The previous command returns an output similar to the following:

```
NAME                          READY   STATUS    RESTARTS   AGE
mysql-5c58b74b44-6lckl        1/1     Running   0          9s
presto-coordinator-vpf7w      1/1     Running   0          9s
presto-worker-26mjb           1/1     Running   0          9s
```

Querying Your Presto Instance

Now that the server is up, let's use Presto to query some data. We'll use the Kubernetes cluster deployed in the previous sections, and the Presto client available on the Presto coordinator. To run it, open a terminal, and run the following command:

```
kubectl exec -it presto-coordinator-vpf7w -n presto -- bash
```

Open the Presto CLI as follows:

```
root@presto-coordinator-vpf7w /]# presto
presto>
```

Listing Catalogs

Presto stores all the available data in catalogs. To list all the stored catalogs, run the following query:

```
show catalogs;
```

You should get the following output, which shows the two configured catalogs (`mysql` and `tpch`), along with the system catalog:

```
Catalog
mysql
system
tpch
(2 rows)

Query 20220921_144917_00003_i6r2z, FINISHED, 1 node
```

Socket Timeout Exception

When you a query in a Presto client, the system may answer with the following error:

```
Error running command: java.net.SocketTimeoutException: timeout
```

This means that the Presto server is initializing, so you need to wait. When Presto is ready, you should be able to get the query output.

Presto follows this for data:

```
Catalog
|--contains zero or more schemas
|--contains zero or more tables or views
```

To explicitly reference a table, follow the dot notation format: `<catalog name>.<schema name>.<table name>`. We'll now look at how to list catalogs, schemas, and tables, and how to query them.

Listing Schemas

All data access is abstracted as databases, schemas, and tables. To look at what schemas are available in a database or a catalog, you can use the `show schemas` command:

```
presto> show schemas from tpch;
        Schema

 information_schema
 sf1
 sf100
 sf1000
 sf10000
 sf100000
 sf300
 sf3000
 sf30000
 tiny
(10 rows)

Query 20210908_045023_00001_j5vw7, FINISHED, 1 node
Splits: 19 total, 19 done (100.00%)
361ms [10 rows, 119B] [27 rows/s, 329B/s]
```

All the schemas define the same set of tables. The schema's name indicates the size of the data: tiny, which is the alias of 0.01, has the smallest amount of data (about 10,000 elements), while sf100000 has the most (about 100 billion elements).

Listing Tables

Every schema contains one or more tables. To list all the tables in the schema, follow the dot notation:

```
presto> show tables from tpch.sf100;
   Table

 customer
 lineitem
 nation
 orders
 part
 partsupp
 region
 supplier
(8 rows)

Query 20210908_045225_00002_j5vw7, FINISHED, 1 node
Splits: 19 total, 19 done (100.00%)
236ms [8 rows, 174B] [33 rows/s, 735B/s]
```

Querying a Table

Now let's query the customer table from the sf100 schema and pull some rows to review. Here again you can follow the dot notation to reference the table.

Before we pull the rows though, let's look at the table's schema. For that you will use show create table, which is the same as describe table in most databases:

```
presto> show create table tpch.sf100.customer;
                Create Table

 CREATE TABLE tpch.sf100.customer (
    "custkey" bigint NOT NULL,
    "name" varchar(25) NOT NULL,
    "address" varchar(40) NOT NULL,
    "nationkey" bigint NOT NULL,
    "phone" varchar(15) NOT NULL,
    "acctbal" double NOT NULL,
    "mktsegment" varchar(10) NOT NULL,
    "comment" varchar(117) NOT NULL
 )
(1 row)

Query 20210908_050304_00011_j5vw7, FINISHED, 1 node
Splits: 1 total, 1 done (100.00%)
43ms [0 rows, 0B] [0 rows/s, 0B/s]
```

Now that you know the fields available in the table, you can select the fields to be returned as a part of your query, instead of select *, which will return all fields, which you may not require. Now let's query some fields from the table to get the customer contact information:

```
select custkey,name,address,phone from tpch.sf100.customer limit 5;

presto> select custkey,name,address,phone from tpch.sf100.customer limit 5;
 custkey  |        name         | address   |    phone

 11250001 | Customer#011250001 | ...       | 24-397-921-1461
 11250002 | Customer#011250002 | ...       | 34-747-594-8280
 11250003 | Customer#011250003 | ...       | 22-456-401-1500
 11250004 | Customer#011250004 | ...       | 24-596-187-3005
 11250005 | Customer#011250005 | ...       | 18-965-501-9572
(5 rows)

Query 20210908_050526_00012_j5vw7, FINISHED, 1 node
Splits: 29 total, 21 done (72.41%)
209ms [51.2K rows, 0B] [245K rows/s, 0B/s]
```

One other way to avoid always having to reference the full dot notation is to leverage the USE <schema> command:

```
presto> use tpch.sf100;
USE
presto:sf100>
```

Until you change the schema or exit this session, you can continue referencing all tables in the tpch.sf100 schema without using the full dot notation. Here is the same query run without the dot notation, after running the USE command:

```
presto:sf100> select custkey,name,address,phone from customer limit 5;
  custkey  |         name        | address     |    phone

 11250001 | Customer#011250001 | ...         | 24-397-921-1461
 11250002 | Customer#011250002 | ...         | 34-747-594-8280
 11250003 | Customer#011250003 | ...         | 22-456-401-1500
 11250004 | Customer#011250004 | ...         | 24-596-187-3005
 11250005 | Customer#011250005 | ...         | 18-965-501-9572
(5 rows)

Query 20210908_050903_00016_j5vw7, FINISHED, 1 node
Splits: 29 total, 18 done (62.07%)
255ms [12.8K rows, 0B] [50.1K rows/s, 0B/s]
```

We have now completed setting up your local cluster and demonstrated the use of the Presto CLI to query data from tables using the dot notation.

Conclusion

In this chapter, you learned how to install Presto using two different approaches: Docker and Kubernetes. Docker permits you to build and run a local instance of Presto without paying particular attention to the software dependencies required on your machine.

Kubernetes allows you to install a local cluster with one Presto coordinator and as many workers as you want. You can also use Kubernetes to configure and deploy additional catalogs to connect to your Presto instance. You also learned how to set up a MySQL pod on Kubernetes and how to connect it to your Presto instance.

You now have set up your machine with a local Presto cluster with a basic configuration using Kubernetes. In Chapter 3, you'll learn how to configure additional connectors and catalogs in your Presto cluster.

Connectors

A Presto connector is a plug-in that connects the Presto engine to an external catalog. Presto connectors are available for a wide variety of data sources, including relational databases, NoSQL databases, and filesystems.

In this chapter, you'll learn how to implement a custom connector. First, we'll describe the concept of the *Service Provider Interface* (SPI) provided by Presto, which defines the interfaces to build custom connectors, types, functions, and system access control in Presto.

Then, we'll focus on the concept of *connectors* and how it's implemented in Presto. Next, you'll learn how to implement a custom connector and an alternative implementation, based on *Apache Thrift*, that enables the communication between Presto and external servers written in any language supported by Thrift, such as Python, PHP, and many more.

Finally, we'll focus on Apache Pinot, which is a real-time distributed datastore, and how to connect it to Presto.

Service Provider Interface

An SPI is an interface you can use to extend a framework with third-party components. Presto implements its own SPI, as shown in Figure 3-1. The *Presto SPI*, which is within the Presto server, manages the communication between the Presto core and the external service providers.

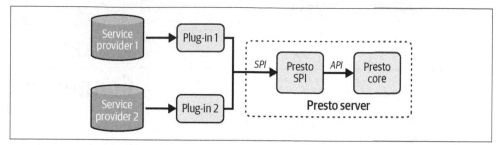

Figure 3-1. The SPI architecture

A service provider, wanting to communicate with Presto, must implement a plug-in module, which interacts with the Presto SPI. Then, the Presto SPI makes the features implemented by the service provider available to the Presto core through an API.

The most popular Presto plug-ins include *connectors*, *types*, *functions*, and *system access control*. In the remainder of this section, we'll give a general overview of each plug-in. For more details, refer to the Presto documentation (*https://oreil.ly/w2wrI*).

Connectors
> A connector enables Presto to interact with external systems for reading and writing data. As we'll see, a connector is responsible for exposing table metadata to Presto, such as schemas, tables, and column definitions, as well as mapping data from the external data source to Presto data types.

Types
> A type is a plug-in that permits you to implement a custom data type in the SQL language. Presto already defines many built-in types, such as BOOLEAN, INTEGER, VARCHAR, and many more. It's not necessary that all the connectors implement a given data type.

Functions
> Presto provides many functions to access data. Example functions include mathematical functions, aggregation, functions on strings, and many more. You can extend the set of available functions by writing your own through the functions' plug-ins.

System access control
> Presto defines some access control policies that permit you to define different roles having different privileges within the Presto cluster. You can write your custom plug-in to specify the system access control. We'll focus on this aspect in Chapter 7.

Connector Architecture

Figure 3-2 shows the flow of a call between Presto and a connector. When a client runs a query in Presto, the Presto coordinator parses and analyzes it (*Parser/Analyzer*) by retrieving useful metadata about the catalogs from each connector (*Metadata API*). Metadata includes the list of available tables, column definitions, and so on. Then, the Presto coordinator plans how to run the query (*Planner*), optimizes it, and defines how to distribute the query among the workers (*Scheduler*) by asking the *Data Location API* for the individual chunks to send to workers. Upon receiving its chunk, a worker runs its task by querying the catalog through to the *Data Stream API*. The result of the query is organized and sent back to the coordinator, which sends it to the client.

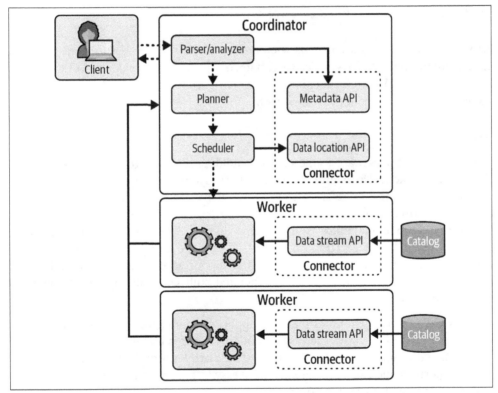

Figure 3-2. The flow of calls between Presto and a connector

Popular Connectors

Presto provides many connectors for different types of catalogs, including relational and nonrelational databases, real-time sources, and other object storage systems, such as the Hadoop Distributed File System (HDFS). The list of the available connectors is continuously increasing; refer to the Presto documentation (*https://oreil.ly/fe3J1*) for more details on the supported connectors. In this book, we'll focus on three connectors: Thrift, Apache Pinot, and Apache Hudi. We'll see Thrift and Apache Pinot in this chapter, and Apache Hudi in Chapter 5. We'll describe Apache Pinot in a separate section of this chapter, given its importance. Table 3-1 provides a brief description of the connectors used in this book.

Table 3-1. The connectors described in this book

Connector	Description of the technology
Thrift	A protocol providing efficient communication between services written in different languages
Apache Pinot	An open source, distributed real-time analytics datastore designed to provide low-latency querying and aggregation of large-scale datasets
Apache Hudi	A data lake platform for storing data in the Hudi table format

In Chapter 2 we saw how to plug a connector into Presto. It is sufficient to add a new configuration file for your catalog, named *mycatalog.properties*, to your `catalog` directory in your Presto installation. Every configuration file must define at least the catalog name (e.g., `connector.name=tpch`).

Thrift

Apache Thrift is a software framework for building scalable cross-language services. Describing Apache Thrift and its architecture is out the scope of this book. For further details, you can refer to the Thrift official documentation (*https://oreil.ly/XmUMd*). However, for our purposes, it's sufficient to know that Apache Thrift includes a compiler that takes as input some abstract data types defined in an Interface Definition Language (IDL). Then, as output, the compiler generates the stub code associated with the input in any of the supported languages, such as Python, PHP, Java, and many more. Use the generated stub code to implement the tasks required by your service.

If you want to implement cross-platform applications, Apache Thrift is an extremely useful tool because it allows the easy creation of services and applications that communicate with each other regardless of language or platform. Thrift is also designed for high performance, and it is actually quite easy to use and very flexible because you can use it for a wide variety of purposes.

Combining Thrift and Presto gives you the ability to easily call Presto from any language supported by Thrift, making it the ideal solution for developing scalable, cross-language applications.

Presto implements the Thrift connector, which you can use as you usually do with the other connectors. Point to the *etc/catalogs/* directory of your Presto coordinator and create a *thrift.properties* file with the following minimal configuration:

```
connector.name=my-thrift-connector
presto.thrift.client.addresses=host:port,host:port
```

Along with the connector name, define the list of addresses of the hosts implementing the stub code generated by the Thrift compiler. For the list of all supported properties, refer to the Presto documentation (*https://oreil.ly/a9NH5*).

To implement the Thrift service, download the Presto IDL service from the book's GitHub repository, under *03/thrift/PrestoThriftService.thrift*, and place it anywhere in your filesystem. Then run the following command to generate the stub code:

```
thrift --gen java PrestoThriftService.thrift
```

The command generates the stub code in Java. Change the keyword `java` to your preferred language to generate the code for that language. You can download the stub code in Java from the book's GitHub repository, under the *03/thrift/thrift-stub-java* directory.

Once you have the stub code, implement the service, depending on the requirements of your external catalog. Use the `presto-thrift-testing-server` module, available on the PrestoDB GitHub repository, as a reference.

Writing a Custom Connector

Imagine that you have a proprietary database and you want to connect it to Presto, but unfortunately none of the available Presto connectors is compatible with your database. In this case, the best choice is to implement your own connector, which maps your database to Presto directly.

In this section, you'll learn how to build a custom connector for Presto from scratch. At a high level, four major components make up a connector:

- Plugin and module
- Configuration
- Metadata
- Input/output

To discuss the components that make up a connector, we'll use the Example HTTP Connector (*https://oreil.ly/Rcnh0*). This is a basic connector that reads CSV files over HTTP. You can look at the source code in the PrestoDB GitHub repository (*https://github.com/prestodb/presto*), under the `presto-example-http` module.

Prerequisites

Because Presto is written in Java, you must write your custom connector in Java. In addition, since Presto is implemented as a standard Maven project, to make your connector project work, install Apache Maven. Also download the Presto JAR file (*https://oreil.ly/NdbsM*) and include it in your project libraries. Optionally, use an IDE to edit your code. In this book, we'll use IntelliJ IDEA (*https://oreil.ly/g—TP*). We recommend using an IDE because it makes it simple to manage a Maven project. If you don't use an IDE, make sure to manually set up all of the environment, including both JDK and the required libraries.

To create a new project, launch IntelliJ IDEA or your favorite IDE, and select File > New > Project > New Project. Then, compile the form, select Maven as the build system, and click Create. Now, add the Presto libraries to your project. If you don't have any JDK installed, select JDK > Download JDK, and then select version 1.8.

When the project is created, add the Presto library to it. Click the project name at the left of the window, and then select Open Module Settings > Libraries > + > Java. Select the Presto JAR file from your filesystem and click OK. The project may also require other external libraries. Add them by selecting Open Module Settings > Libraries > + > From Maven and then searching for the required libraries.

To load the Example HTTP Connector in IntelliJ IDEA, download the Presto source code (*https://github.com/prestodb/presto*) and load it by selecting File > New > Project > New Project from existing sources > Import project from external model > Maven.

Plugin and Module

The plugin and module specify the top-level classes that make up your connector, allowing Presto to initialize your catalog. In the Example HTTP Connector, the main classes involved at this level are `ExamplePlugin`, `ExampleConnectorFactory`, `Example Module`, `ExampleConnector`, and `ExampleHandleResolver`, as shown in Figure 3-3.

> **How to Name Classes**
>
> There is no precise rule in naming the implemented classes. However, we recommend naming a class with the name of the connector (`Example` in the case of the Example HTTP Connector) followed by the implemented interface (e.g., `Plugin`).

In the figure, the classes involved at the plugin and module level appear in black boxes. The gray boxes show the classes created, configured, pointed to, or returned by these classes.

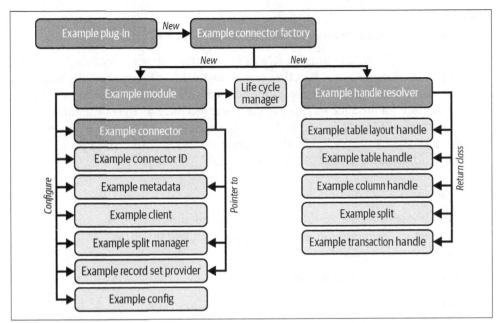

Figure 3-3. Main classes involved at the level of plugin and module

ExamplePlugin

This class implements the Presto `Plugin` interface, which tells Presto the features that this plug-in has. Since this example is a connector, `ExamplePlugin` only implements the `getConnectorFactory()` method and returns the `ExampleConnectorFactory`. If this plug-in implemented other functionalities, such as functions and types, you should implement them here through other methods.

ExampleConnectorFactory

A `ConnectorFactory` is the base interface aiming at creating connectors for a particular provider. The `ExampleConnectorFactory` class implements the Presto `Connector Factory` interface and provides the following basic classes:

`getName()`
> Returns the name of the connector, *example-http*: The connector name uniquely identifies this connector in a Presto installation. Use the connector name defined here when you create the Presto catalog, as described in Chapter 2.

`getHandleResolver()`
> Creates a new `ExampleHandleResolver` object, which tells Presto what classes to use for this connector.

```
create()
```
Creates the modules required to run the connector.

Presto uses Google Guice (*https://oreil.ly/uxVjt*) for dependency injection. Explaining this project (and dependency injection in general) is out of scope for this book, but in short, you define the module the connector requires (which we will see next), and then you create an instance of it using the injector. Guice analyzes the module and what classes are needed, creating instances as necessary. Guice reports any missing dependencies on startup, and then the program crashes. See the Guice project documentation (*https://oreil.ly/mVFdK*) for more details.

ExampleModule

This class implements the `Module` interface defined through Google Guice. Within the `configure()` method, you must configure any class that uses Google Guice, as shown in the following code:

```
public void configure(Binder binder)
{
  binder.bind(ExampleConnector.class).in(Scopes.SINGLETON);
  ...
}
```

ExampleConnector

This class implements the Presto `Connector` interface and lays out the connector's supported features. Presto instantiates this class with the following four objects: `LifeCycleManager` and a custom implementation of the `MetaData`, `SplitManager`, and `RecordSetProvider` interfaces.

The `ExampleConnector` class implements the methods to return the instantiated objects, as well as the methods to begin a transaction and shut down:

```
public class ExampleConnector implements Connector
{
@Inject
public ExampleConnector(
        LifeCycleManager lifeCycleManager,
        ExampleMetadata metadata,
        ExampleSplitManager splitManager,
        ExampleRecordSetProvider recordSetProvider){...}

public ConnectorTransactionHandle
    beginTransaction(IsolationLevel isolationLevel, boolean readOnly){...}
public ConnectorMetadata
    getMetadata(ConnectorTransactionHandle transactionHandle){...}
public ConnectorSplitManager getSplitManager(){...}
public ConnectorRecordSetProvider getRecordSetProvider(){...}
public final void shutdown(){...}
}
```

The @Inject decorator before the constructor tells Google Guice to add the class to the injection's dependency.

ExampleHandleResolver

This class implements the Presto ConnectorHandleResolver interface and is used by Presto to determine the implemented handles. At a minimum, users must provide an implementation of the following handles: ConnectorTableHandle, ConnectorTable LayoutHandle, ColumnHandle, ConnectorTransactionHandle, and ConnectorSplit. These classes are explained in more detail later in this section.

For each implemented handle, ExampleHandleResolver must define a method that returns it:

```
@Override
    public Class<? extends ConnectorTableHandle> getTableHandleClass()
    {
        return ExampleTableHandle.class;
    }
```

Configuration

The configuration includes classes for specifying catalog configurations, such as external database URLs and credentials, as well as session properties. There are three kinds of Presto classes you will typically see related to configuration: connector properties (ExampleConfig), session properties (SessionProperties), and table properties (TableProperties).

ExampleConfig

Connector properties provide static information used by your connector, typically items like connection information such as URIs and login information. The Example Config class defines the methods to set and get the properties that you'll use in the catalog configuration file for Presto, such as *example-http.properties*.

The Example HTTP Connector defines the ExampleConfig class to implement the properties of the connector. For example, to set a property named metadata-uri, the ExampleConfig class defines the following method:

```
@Config("metadata-uri")
public ExampleConfig setMetadata(URI metadata)
{
  this.metadata = metadata;
  return this;
}
```

The @Config annotation specifies the property name to set in *example-http.proper-ties*, while other annotations on the getters can enforce restrictions on the values.

For example, @NotNull tells Presto that this configuration value cannot be null, or @Size(min = 1) enforces that users cannot set any value less than one.

SessionProperties

Session properties are items specified by a user for each client session, generally used to tweak configuration settings based on the types of queries a user wants to run or to enable experimental features. Set session properties via the shell as follows:

```
SET SESSION connectorname.propertyname = 'value'
```

The Example HTTP Connector does not define any session property. However, to understand how session properties work, we define a simple session property, LOG_VERBOSITY, which enables logs if set to true.

The constructor of ExampleSessionProperties creates a list of all available properties. Each property has a name, description, SQL data type, Java data type, default value, whether or not the session property is hidden, and encoder/decoder functions. For example, create the LOG_VERBOSITY session property as follows:

```
PropertyMetadata<Boolean> s1 = booleanProperty(
LOG_VERBOSITY,
"Set to true to enable log verbosity.",
true,
false);
```

You create a property using the PropertyMetadata constructor. To check whether the LOG_VERBOSITY session property is enabled, ExampleSessionProperties defines the following method:

```
public static boolean isLogVerbosityEnabled(ConnectorSession session)
{
  return session.getProperty(LOG_VERBOSITY, Boolean.class);
}
```

TableProperties

Table properties are properties attached to a specific table of your external system, such as the properties to specify how the table would be partitioned. The structure of a table property class is similar to that of the session property (look for an example at HiveTableProperties (*https://oreil.ly/eVkCj*) defined by the Hive connector to get an idea).

Use table properties for table definitions in the WITH clause:

```
CREATE TABLE foo (a BIGINT)
WITH
(
 myTableProperty = 'value',
```

```
    myOtherTableProperty = 'othervalue'
);
```

Metadata

The metadata includes classes that define the data model, as well as handles that expose the data model to Presto. In addition, to manage the data model and its handles, you must implement two classes: `Metadata` and `Client`. Figure 3-4 shows the main classes involved at the level of metadata for the Example HTTP Connector.

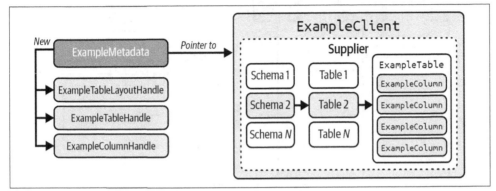

Figure 3-4. Main classes involved at the level of metadata

`ExampleClient` contains a `Supplier` map that represents the data model. We'll see the details of the data model later in this chapter. `ExampleMetadata` contains a pointer to `ExampleClient` and creates a new instance of `ExampleTableLayoutHandle`, `ExampleTableHandle`, and `ExampleColumnHandle`, whenever needed.

Data model

Presto represents data using a relational model; thus every Presto connector must expose data through a relational model, although the original representation of data provided by the connector could be different. A relational model represents data in *schemas*, *tables*, and *columns*. Each schema can have one or more tables, and each table can have one or more columns. The actual data of each table can reside in one or more physical objects.

In your connector, you must define at least the `Table` and `Column` classes as Plain Old Java Objects (POJOs) decorated with a `JsonCreator` annotation. This annotation is used by Presto to serialize the POJO to a JSON object, which is passed around between the coordinator and worker nodes.

Handles

To make Presto access the classes of the data model, you must also implement their relative handles that are the classes that Presto uses in its processing, such as parsing, planning, and so on: TableHandle, ColumnHandle, and TableLayoutHandle.

Figure 3-5 shows the flow of calls to retrieve a table handle in the Example HTTP Connector.

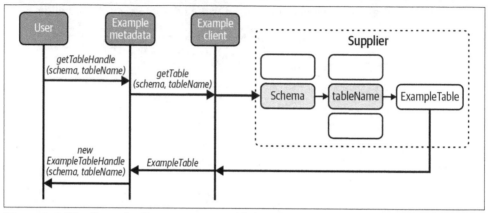

Figure 3-5. The flow of calls to retrieve a table handle in the Example HTTP Connector

The user starts the flow by calling the getTableHandle() method of the ExampleMeta data object, by specifying the *schema* and the *tableName* for which to retrieve the ExampleTableHandle. The ExampleMetadata object, which stores a pointer to the ExampleClient object, translates this call into a call to the getTable() of the Example Client object. The ExampleClient object extracts the ExampleTable and returns it to the ExampleMetadata object to check whether the returned object is null. If it is not null, the ExampleMetadata object creates a new instance of ExampleTableHandle and returns it to the client.

ExampleMetadata

This class implements the ConnectorMetadata interface that contains all the methods for exposing schemas, tables, and column information to Presto. Implement each of these methods based on how you have modeled your external system to a relational model for Presto.

ExampleClient

This class implements the functionalities for fetching schemas, tables, and column definitions. In the Example HTTP Connector, the implementation of this class is pretty lightweight since it is an example connector. In a real connector, your client would typically make API calls to your external system to map its metadata model to

Presto's relational metadata model. As shown in Figure 3-4, `ExampleClient` maintains a map to represent the logical structure of the catalog.

Input/Output

Input/output refers to classes that read and/or write data from your external system into Presto.

Conceptually, to read records from a table, first split the table scan into multiple split objects that can be run in parallel by the Presto workers. Then, for each split, create a record set for the split, and the record set contains a cursor that iterates over rows of data fed to Presto.

Figure 3-6 shows the main classes involved at the level of input/output for the Example HTTP Connector that implement only the reading operation.

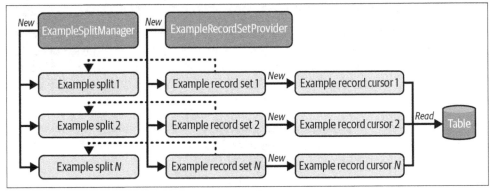

Figure 3-6. Main classes involved at the input/output level

`ExampleSplitManager` creates N multiple `ExampleSplit` objects, where N is the number of sources in the table. For each split, `ExampleRecordSetProvider` creates a new `ExampleRecordSet`. Each `ExampleRecordSet` object maintains a pointer to the `ExampleSplit` it's associated with. In addition, each `ExampleRecordSet` object creates a new `ExampleRecordCursor` object that performs the raw reading operation from the table.

Page Source Provider and Page Sink Provider

Optionally, in addition to `RecordSetProvider` you can implement a `PageSourceProvider`, which is another interface for providing pages of data to Presto (versus individual records), and the `PageSinkProvider` for writing data.

ExampleSplitManager

This class implements the ConnectorSplitManager interface and has one method, getSplits(), which specifies how to split the tables provided by the connector into multiple pieces that can be read in parallel by Presto workers. This method receives as input a ConnectorSession (which can be used to access your session properties), a TableLayoutHandle that is being scanned, and the context. Presto takes the splits returned by the getSplits() method and passes them to the RecordSetProvider.

ExampleSplit

This class implements the ConnectorSplit interface and is associated with a specific chunk of the overall table. Like the metadata classes, it is a Jackson POJO object containing the schema, table, and URI to read.

ExampleRecordSetProvider and ExampleRecordSet

This ExampleRecordSetProvider implements the ConnectorRecordSetProvider interface and creates a RecordSet from the given split via the getRecordSet() method. It also includes a list of columns that are expected to be read from the table and in the record set. These lists of columns would be the columns a user is selecting, for example through SELECT *.

The ExampleRecordSet implements the RecordSet interface and is used to instantiate an ExampleRecordCursor, which iterates over the split to provide rows of data.

ExampleRecordCursor

This class implements the RecordCursor interface and performs the raw reading operations. The Example HTTP Connector reads CSV files. Thus, the ExampleRecord Cursor class must implement the methods to iterate over the columns and rows of the file to return the desired values.

When an ExampleRecordCursor object is instantiated, it loads all the lines of the source file into an iterator of strings:

```
public ExampleRecordCursor(
    List<ExampleColumnHandle> columnHandles,
    ByteSource byteSource)
{
    ...
    lines = byteSource.asCharSource(UTF_8).readLines().iterator();
    ...
}
```

Depending on the operation to run, ExampleRecordCursor iterates over this iterator to extract the desired information. For example, while reading the CSV file, use the following method to advance the next position:

```
public boolean advanceNextPosition()
{
    if (!lines.hasNext()) {
        return false;
    }
    String line = lines.next();
    fields = LINE_SPLITTER.splitToList(line);

    return true;
}
```

The LINE_SPLITTER object is a static member of ExampleRecordCursor and simply separates the columns of the line:

```
private static final Splitter LINE_SPLITTER = Splitter.on(",").trimResults();
```

Deploying Your Connector

To deploy your connector, build your project with Maven using the *presto-plugin* packaging. To configure the *pom.xml* file, view the *pom.xml* file of the presto-example-http project and use it as a starting point, modifying the project name and dependencies as needed.

You have two options to build your project: using the command line or using IntelliJ. When using Maven from the command line, simply run the following command from your project directory: mvn package. If you use IntelliJ, follow these steps:

1. Open the Maven Projects sidebar on the right of your project.

2. Select your project and navigate to the Lifecycle section.

3. Double-click the package.

Once the package is built, copy the produced *target* folder and its contents to your Presto installation plug-ins directory. Then, add the catalog for your connector in the *etc/catalogs* directory, and restart Presto.

Apache Pinot

Apache Pinot, or Pinot for short, is a real-time distributed online analytical processing (OLAP) datastore, aiming to provide ultra-low-latency analytics, even when handling extreme high throughput. You can use Pinot to ingest data sources of all kinds, including *real-time* data sources, such as Apache Kafka, and *batch* data sources, such as Hadoop HDFS. In a real-time analytics scenario, Pinot is one of the components of a data lakehouse and is usually connected to an Amazon S3 bucket. We will describe how to set up a data lakehouse in Chapter 5.

This chapter focuses on Apache Pinot because it is well suited for real-time use cases involving high-dimensional data. In addition, Pinot's fast querying capabilities make it an ideal data source for Presto. As a result, when used together, Pinot and Presto provide a powerful platform for fast and efficient analytical queries on large-scale datasets.

Presto provides a connector to Pinot. In this section, we'll see how to configure Pinot to work with Presto. Describing Pinot and its architecture is out of the scope of this book. You can refer to the Pinot official documentation (*https://oreil.ly/gkblA*) for further details.

Setting Up and Configuring Presto

Pinot provides neither full ANSI SQL support nor standard database access API support like ODBC/JDBC. Connecting Pinot to Presto overcomes this deficit because users can use the Presto features to access Pinot, including the ANSI SQL and ODBC/JDBC support.

In addition, there are two benefits of connecting Presto to Pinot:

- The same SQL code can be used for data in Pinot as well as a data lakehouse or other data sources. For example, you may want to run a query on the new real-time data, but then run the same query on historical data in a lakehouse (a.k.a. "One SQL to rule them all").

- Federated queries across Pinot and another data source provide more correlation or insight.

Setting up Pinot

We'll configure Pinot as a node of the Kubernetes cluster deployed in Chapter 2. To preserve resources in our local machine, we'll deploy Pinot in a single node. In a realistic production environment, Pinot is deployed in a cluster of nodes.

The code used in this section is available in the directory *03/presto-and-pinot*, which contains the Pinot configuration file and the Presto configuration files.

Configuring Pinot

Pinot is composed of four main modules: *controller*, *broker*, *servers*, and *zookeeper*. The description of each module is out of the scope of this book. For this book, it's sufficient to know that the modules are organized in a cluster, and the controller is the orchestrator, like the Presto coordinator is in Presto.

To deploy Pinot on your machine, follow the official Pinot documentation. However, if you don't have enough resources (at least 16 GB of RAM) on your machine to run both Pinot and Presto, follow the procedure described in this section, which describes how to deploy all the Pinot modules in a single pod (*pinot-deployment.yaml*):

```
apiVersion: v1
kind: ReplicationController
metadata:
  name: pinot
spec:
  replicas: 1
  template:
    metadata:
      labels:
        app: pinot
    spec:
      containers:
        - name: pinot
          image: apachepinot/pinot:latest
          command: ["/opt/pinot/bin/pinot-admin.sh"]
          args: ["QuickStart", "-type", "batch"]
          ports:
            - containerPort: 9000
          resources:
            requests:
              memory: "2Gi"
            limits:
              memory: "2Gi"
```

Use a `ReplicationController` to deploy your Pinot cluster. After installing the `apachepinot/pinot:latest` image, the script runs the command `/opt/pinot/bin/pinot-admin.sh QuickStart -type batch`, which installs all the components and adds some sample tables to the database. Refer to the official documentation for further details and examples. Depending on your machine's requirements, adjust your resources under the `resources` section.

Configuring Presto with Pinot

To make Presto work with Pinot, add Pinot as a new catalog to the Presto configuration. Add a new entry to *presto-config-map.yaml*:

```
pinot.properties: |
    connector.name=pinot
    pinot.controller-urls=pinot:9000
    pinot.controller-rest-service=pinot:9000
```

Refer to the Presto documentation (*https://oreil.ly/UoFjt*) for additional configuration options.

To configure the coordinator and the workers with the Pinot catalog, add a new entry to `volumeMount` in both *presto-coordinator.yaml* and *presto-workers.yaml*:

```
containers:
 - name:
   volumeMounts:
    - name: pinot
      mountPath: "/opt/presto/etc/catalog/pinot.properties"
      subPath: pinot.properties
  ...
volumes:
 - name: pinot
   configMap:
     name: presto-config
     items:
      - key: "pinot.properties"
        path: "pinot.properties"
```

Presto-Pinot Querying in Action

Now that the configuration is up, we'll run two sample queries. Use the Presto client available in the Presto coordinator to run your queries.

First, list all the available tables available in Pinot:

```
presto> show tables from pinot.default;
           Table
-------------------------
 airlinestats
 baseballstats
 billing
 dimbaseballteams
 githubcomplextypeevents
 githubevents
 starbucksstores
(7 rows)

Query 20221019_100155_00006_47zex, FINISHED, 1 node
Splits: 19 total, 19 done (100.00%)
0:17 [7 rows, 217B] [0 rows/s, 12B/s]
```

Use the baseballstats table for the next query. To understand how Presto runs a query, use the EXPLAIN operator before your query. For example, to list the number of times a player name is repeated in the table, run the following query:

```
EXPLAIN
 SELECT playerName, count(1) \
 FROM pinot.default.baseballStats \
 GROUP BY playerName;
```

The command produces a long log that includes the nested calls to the Presto components. Presto propagates the query from the upper layer (TableScan) to the bottom layer (PinotColumnHandle and GeneratedPinotQuery). The following piece of code shows the flow of calls in pseudocode:

```
TableScan ->
 TableHandle ->
  expectedColumnHandles ->
   PinotColumnHandle{columnName="playerName", ...}
   PinotColumnHandle{columnName="count", ...}
  layout ->
   PinotTableHandle ->
    expectedColumnHandles ->
     PinotColumnHandle{columnName="playerName", ...}
     PinotColumnHandle{columnName="count", ...}
    pinotQuery ->
     GeneratedPinotQuery
     {
      query=SELECT "playerName", count(*)
            FROM baseballStats
            GROUP BY "playerName"
            LIMIT 10000,
     }
```

Conclusion

In this chapter, you learned how to implement a custom connector in Presto, both using the Presto SPI and Thrift.

SPI requires that you write your custom connector in Java by implementing different classes, including four main components: plugin and module, configuration, and input/output. For each component, you must implement some classes, which enable the communication between your catalog and the Presto core. Although your original catalog is not relational, your custom connector must expose data using a relational data model.

In addition, you learned how to write a custom connector using Apache Thrift, a software framework that enables developers to build scalable cross-language services. Thanks to the Thrift connector, Presto communicates with external services written in languages other than Java.

You also learned how to connect Apache Pinot, a real-time distributed OLAP datastore, to Presto. You have set up your machine with a Pinot instance running on Kubernetes and connected it with the Presto cluster you deployed in Chapter 2.

In Chapter 4, you'll learn some advanced techniques to connect a client to Presto.

Client Connectivity

A Presto client is a process that queries Presto and shows the query results for a number of purposes, such as data analytics, ad hoc queries, and many more. Presto provides a variety of clients, written in different programming languages, including REST API, R, Python, JDBC, Node.js, and ODBC.

This chapter is organized into two parts. In the first part, you'll learn how to deploy a Presto client. Although you can deploy a Presto client as a separate process running on an existing cluster node, in this chapter, you'll implement the client on a different node to simulate an external application accessing the cluster. We'll focus on implementing a client in the REST API, Python, R, JDBC, Node.js, and ODBC. You can easily extend the described procedure to the other programming languages supported by Presto.

In the second part, you'll implement a practical web service in Python, querying Presto and showing the results in a simple dashboard. The goal of this example is to illustrate the potentialities of a Presto client.

Setting Up the Environment

To add a Presto client as a node of the Presto cluster, first you must set up the environment. Deploy the following three components already implemented in Chapter 3:

- Presto client
- Docker image that contains your Presto client
- Kubernetes node that runs the Docker image in the Presto cluster

The code used in this section is available in the *04* directory of the book's repository, which contains the configuration files for all the described Presto clients.

Presto Client

The Presto client connects to Presto, runs queries, and shows the results. You can write your Presto client in your preferred language. Save the code into a directory that will be mounted in the Kubernetes node as a separate volume. Optionally, write a web application or a service that permits access over HTTP. We'll see how to deploy a client web service later in this chapter. Alternatively, use the terminal to access your Presto client.

Docker Image

The Docker image contains the environment needed to run your Presto client. Use the following template for the *Dockerfile*:

```
FROM <basic_image>
RUN apt-get update && \
<install required libraries>
```

For example, to build the image for the R client, write the following *Dockerfile*:

```
FROM r-base
RUN apt-get update && \
apt install -y build-essential libcurl4-gnutls-dev libxml2-dev libssl-dev
RUN R -e "install.packages('RPresto')"
```

To build your Docker image, run the following command in a terminal:

```
docker build -t client-presto .
```

Kubernetes Node

To deploy a Kubernetes node in the Presto cluster, write a *.yaml* configuration file that simply wraps the Docker image:

```
apiVersion: apps/v1
kind: Deployment
metadata:
  name: my-client
  labels:
    app: my-client
spec:
  replicas: 1
  selector:
    matchLabels:
      app: my-client
  template:
    metadata:
      labels:
        app: my-client
    spec:
      containers:
```

```
      - name: my-client
        image:  client-presto:latest
        imagePullPolicy: Never
        command: [ "sleep" ]
        args: [ "infinity" ]
```

The command `sleep infinity` makes sure that Kubernetes keeps your client alive. Alternatively, if your client runs a service, modify the configuration code to deploy the service.

To run custom scripts in your Docker container, mount a local volume:

```
spec:
 containers:
 - name: client
   # add details based on the client type
   volumeMounts:
    - name: scripts
      mountPath: "/path/in/the/container"

 volumes:
  - name: scripts
    hostPath:
      path: "/path/to/scripts/in/the/host"
```

Deploy the client by running the following command:

```
kubectl apply -f client.yaml --namespace presto
```

Once you have deployed your client, log in to it and run the scripts in the mounted directory.

Mounting Warning

Use the `volumeMount` option while writing your code. In a production environment, wrap the implemented app directly in the Docker image instead of mounting it in a separate directory in your Kubernetes *.yaml* file.

Connectivity to Presto

This section gives an overview of how to use the existing client libraries to set up a connection to the Presto cluster. We'll use the different programming languages supported by Presto. Download the running example in your preferred language from the book's GitHub repository, under the directory *04/<language>_client*. Feel free to skip the languages that don't interest you.

REST API

The Presto coordinator includes an HTTP server that supports a REST API endpoint. All the communications between the client and the Presto coordinator use the HTTP protocol. To run a Presto client using a REST API, specify at least the URL to the Presto coordinator, the query, and a minimal header that includes the catalog and the schema to query:

```
curl -d "SELECT * FROM customer LIMIT 5" \
  --request POST \
  -s "presto-coordinator:8080/<endpoint>" \
  -H "X-Presto-User: client" \
  -H "X-Presto-Catalog: tpch" \
  -H "X-Presto-Schema: sf1"
```

Specify the user using `-H "X-Presto-User: client"`. By default, Presto accepts any user, so write any name. In Chapter 7, you'll see how to configure specific users in Presto.

If the call to the REST API is successful, Presto returns a JSON object where the `nextUri` key is set. Run another call to Presto using the value corresponding to the `nextUri` key as the URL. You'll see an example for this later in this section.

The REST API provides you with many endpoints, such as the following:

`/v1/node`
> To get information about a node.

`/v1/statement`
> To run queries.

`/v1/query`
> To get metrics on the most recent queries. Optionally, specify the query ID to get information about a specific query.

`/v1/thread`
> To get information about a thread.

`/v1/task`
> To get information about a task.

Iterate the previous call to Presto until the `nextUri` key is absent in the response JSON object. If the last call is successful, the returned object contains the query results as the value of the `data` key.

```
curl -s "URL contained in nextUri"
```

The following code shows a complete example of a call to the REST API in Python:

1. Run the first call to the REST API:

```
import requests
import time

url = "http://presto-coordinator:8080/v1/statement"

headers = {
    "X-Presto-User" : "client", \
    "X-Presto-Catalog": "tpch", \
    "X-Presto-Schema": "sf1"
    }

sql = "SELECT * FROM customer LIMIT 5"

resp = requests.post(url, headers=headers, data=sql)
json_resp = resp.json()
```

2. Iterate over the `nextUri` key until it's absent. Use `time.sleep(0.5)` to wait for data. Increase this value if your client does not receive any data.

```
while 'nextUri' in json_resp:
  time.sleep(0.5)
  new_url = json_resp['nextUri']
  resp = requests.get(new_url)
  json_resp = resp.json()
```

3. Get the final data:

```
data = json_resp['data']
for i in range(0, len(data)):
  print(data[i])
```

The Presto REST API provides many additional parameters. Read the Presto documentation (*https://oreil.ly/JjAye*) for more details.

Python

Install the `presto-python-client` library. In your *Dockerfile*, run the following command:

```
pip install presto-python-client
```

Then, connect to Presto as follows:

```
import prestodb
conn=prestodb.dbapi.connect(
    host='presto-coordinator',
    port=8080,
    user='client',
    catalog='tpch',
    schema='sf1',
)
```

To run a query, retrieve the cursor:

```
cur = conn.cursor()
cur.execute('SELECT * FROM customer LIMIT 5')
rows = cur.fetchall()
```

R

Install the RPresto library. In your *Dockerfile*, run the following command:

```
RUN R -e "install.packages('RPresto')"
```

To query Presto in R, first import the required libraries:

```
library(RPresto)
library(DBI)
```

Then connect to the Presto server:

```
con <- DBI::dbConnect(
  drv = RPresto::Presto(),
  host = "presto-coordinator",
  port = 8080,
  user = "r-client",
  catalog = "tpch",
  schema = "sf1"
)
```

To run a query, use the DBI::dbGetQuery() function:

```
DBI::dbGetQuery(con, "SELECT * FROM customer LIMIT 5")
```

JDBC

Use the Presto JDBC driver com.facebook.presto.jdbc.PrestoDriver. If you use Maven, add the following dependencies to your *pom.xml* file:

```
<dependencies>
 <dependency>
  <groupId>com.facebook.presto</groupId>
  <artifactId>presto-jdbc</artifactId>
  <version>0.276</version>
 </dependency>
</dependencies>
```

If you don't use Maven, download the *presto-jdbc-0.276.jar* file from the Presto website and add it to the classpath of your Java application. Replace the Presto version with the most recent version of Presto (0.276 at the time of writing this chapter).

In your main Java application, define the URL to the Presto server and connect to Presto through a Connection:

```
import java.sql.DriverManager;
import java.sql.Connection;
import java.sql.SQLException;

String url = "jdbc:presto://presto-coordinator:8080/tpch/sf1";

try {
 Class.forName("com.facebook.presto.jdbc.PrestoDriver");

 Connection connection =
          DriverManager.getConnection(url, "test", null);
}
catch(SQLException e){
 e.printStackTrace();
}
catch(ClassNotFoundException e){
 e.printStackTrace();
}
```

In the URL string, specify the catalog (tpch) and the schema (sf1). Then run your queries:

```
String sql = "SELECT * FROM customer LIMIT 5";

try{
 Statement statement = connection.createStatement();
 ResultSet rs = statement.executeQuery(sql);
 while (rs.next()) {
     System.out.println(rs.getString(1));
 }
}
catch(SQLException e){
 e.printStackTrace();
}
```

The example prints the first column for each result in the query's result set.

Node.js

Install the presto-client library:

```
npm install -g presto-client
```

In your main JavaScript application, import the library and create a new Client() object:

```
var presto = require('presto-client');
var client = new presto.Client({
 user: 'myuser',
 'host': 'http://presto-coordinator',
 port: '8080'
});
```

Then execute any query:

```
client.execute({
  query:   'SELECT * FROM customer LIMIT 5',
  catalog: 'tpch',
  schema:  'sf1',
  source:  'nodejs-client',
  data:    function(error, data, columns, stats){ console.log(data); },
  success: function(error, stats){console.log(stats);},
  error:   function(error){console.log(error);}
});
```

ODBC

Open Database Connectivity (ODBC) is a standard database access method that enables applications to access data in a variety of database formats. Many database vendors, such as Microsoft, Oracle, and IBM, provide ODBC proprietary drivers to connect to any ODBC-compliant database, regardless of the database's underlying structure or format.

To implement a Presto ODBC client, first you must install an ODBC driver. In this book, we use CData (*https://oreil.ly/qaRxM*).

To make the driver work, first install the unixodbc, unixodbc-dev, and tdsodbc libraries. For example, in Ubuntu, run the following command:

```
apt-get install -y unixodbc unixodbc-dev tdsodbc
```

Next, download the CData driver for Presto (Unix version), install the package, and activate the license:

```
dpkg -i PrestoODBCDriverforUnix.deb
cd /opt/cdata/cdata-odbc-driver-for-presto/bin/
./install-license.sh
```

Then install the client library in your preferred language to access Presto through the ODBC driver. For example, in Python, install pyodbc:

```
pip install pyodbc
```

In your ODBC client application, connect to the Presto database:

```
conn=pyodbc.connect("DRIVER=CData ODBC Driver for Presto;\
server=presto-coordinator;\
Port=8080;user=client;\
catalog=tpch;schema=sf1")
```

Then execute any query:

```
cur = conn.cursor()
cur.execute('SELECT * FROM customer LIMIT 5')
rows = cur.fetchall()
print(rows)
```

Other Presto Client Libraries

Presto supports many other languages, including C, Go, PHP, and Ruby. The procedure to build your client in any of these languages is essentially the same. Refer to the Presto GitHub profile (*https://oreil.ly/o_mdE*) to download the template for a specific client. For example, use the Go client in the Presto GitHub profile's Go repository (*https://oreil.ly/oh9Ss*).

Building a Client Dashboard in Python

This section describes a practical example of how to implement a simple dashboard querying Presto in Python from scratch. The dashboard is a web application, which connects to Presto, runs a sample query, and shows the outputs of the query in two separate graphs.

The code described in this section is available in the book's GitHub repository, under the directory *04/client-app*.

Setting Up the Client

The dashboard runs as a Kubernetes node, which exposes an HTTP service to access the dashboard. We'll implement the dashboard using the following Python libraries:

Streamlit
    Transforms Python scripts into web applications very quickly

Altair
    A Python library for data visualization

Pandas
    A popular Python library for dataset manipulation

To configure the client, perform the following steps:

1. Write the *Dockerfile* that copies the app code to the Docker image, installs the required libraries, exposes the Streamlit listening port, and runs the app:

    ```
    FROM python:3.8.6
    WORKDIR /app

    COPY app .
    ```

```
RUN pip install --upgrade pip
RUN pip install presto-python-client
RUN pip install streamlit altair pandas

EXPOSE 8501

CMD ["./run.sh"]
```

The *run.sh* script simply launches the Streamlit server:

```
#!/bin/bash
streamlit run app.py --browser.serverAddress 0.0.0.0
```

2. Build the Docker image by running the following command from the directory where the *Dockerfile* is located:

```
docker build -t client-app .
```

3. Wrap the `client-app` Docker image into a Kubernetes node, using the procedure that you have already followed for the Python client. Do not mount an external volume since the application is already available from the Docker image. In addition, make the web server port available for external access.

```
spec:
 containers:
 - name: client-app
   image:  client-app:latest
   ...
   ports:
     - containerPort: 8501
```

4. Build a service for the web application:

```
---
apiVersion: v1
kind: Service
metadata:
  name: client-service
  labels:
    app: client-service
spec:
  ports:
    - port: 8501
      protocol: TCP
      targetPort: 8501
  type: LoadBalancer
  selector:
    app: client-app
```

The service exposes the same port as the original web server. In addition, it uses a `LoadBalancer` to make the service available outside of the Kubernetes cluster.

5. Deploy the client-app node in the `presto` cluster:

```
kubectl apply -f client-app.yaml --namespace presto
```

6. Finally, open your browser and point to *http://localhost:8501* to access the web application.

Building the Dashboard

The client dashboard is a web server that connects to Presto, runs a sample query, and shows the outputs as graphs. The objective of this app is to demonstrate the potentialities of building a client app rather than building a complete example of data analytics.

The code of the client dashboard is available under *04/client-app/app* of the GitHub repository for the book. The code is organized into a single script named *app.py*, which runs the web server as a Streamlit web server. In detail, the app performs the following operations:

- Connecting to and querying Presto
- Preparing the results of the query
- Building the first graph
- Building the second graph

Connecting to and querying Presto

First, the app imports all the required libraries:

```
import prestodb
import altair as alt
import pandas as pd
import streamlit as st
```

Then the app connects to Presto using the `prestodb` library. Use the code described in "Python" on page 61 to perform the connection.

Resources Warning

If your local machine does not have enough resources to manage a big dataset, use the `tiny` schema from the TPC-H catalog when you specify the connection parameters to Presto. The `tiny` schema contains about 10,000 sample data items.

The app runs a query that lists the number of items shipped by date from the TPC-H catalog and orders them by oldest shipping date:

```
query = """SELECT
    count(*) as nitems,
    shipdate
FROM
    lineitem
GROUP BY shipdate
ORDER BY shipdate ASC
    """
```

Preparing the results of the query

The app stores the result of the query in a Pandas DataFrame:

```
cur.execute(query)
df = pd.DataFrame(cur.fetchall(), columns=['nitems', 'shipdate'])
```

To build the final graphs, the app extracts some information from shipdate:

```
df['shipdate'] = pd.to_datetime(df['shipdate'])
df['dayofweek'] = df['shipdate'].dt.day_name()
df['year'] = df['shipdate'].dt.year
df['month'] = df['shipdate'].dt.month_name()
df['weekofyear'] = df['shipdate'].dt.isocalendar().week
```

The extracted information includes the day of the week (from Sunday to Saturday), year, month, and week of the year (a progressive number from 1 to 53).

Building the first graph

The first graph focuses on 1992 and shows a line for each week of the year, related to the number of shipped items organized by day of the week:

```
df_1992 = df[df['year'] == 1992 ]
```

The graph is composed of two parts. The first part of the graph shows a line for each week of the year:

```
days_of_weeks = ['Sunday', ... ,'Saturday']
bar = alt.Chart(df_1992).mark_line().encode(
    x = alt.X('dayofweek:O',
      sort=days_of_weeks,title=''
    ),
    y = alt.Y('nitems:Q', title='nitems'),
    color = alt.Color('weekofyear:N',
      scale=alt.Scale(range=['#C8C8C8']),
      legend=None
    )
)
```

The second part of the graph shows the average value of the number of shipped items over all the weeks:

```
mean = alt.Chart(df_1992).mark_line(color='black').encode(
    x = alt.X('dayofweek:O',
```

```
        sort=days_of_week,
        title=''
    ),
    y = alt.Y('weekly_count:Q', title=''),
).transform_aggregate(
    weekly_count = 'mean(nitems)',
    groupby=['dayofweek']
)
```

Finally, the app combines the two parts to build the final graph:

```
chart1 = (bar + mean).properties(
    width=300,
    height=300,
    title='Number of shipped items in 1992')
)
st.altair_chart(chart1)
```

We use the `st.altair_chart()` function to build the graph. Figure 4-1 shows the resulting graph.

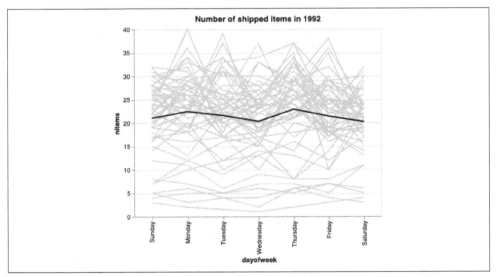

Figure 4-1. Number of shipped items in 1992 organized by week

Building the second graph

The second graph shows a calendar heatmap, with years on the x-axis and months on the y-axis:

```
chart2 = alt.Chart(df).mark_rect().encode(
    x = alt.X('year:O'),
    y = alt.Y('month:O',
    sort=days_of_weeks
    ),
```

```
    color = alt.Color(
      'nitems:Q',
       scale=alt.Scale(range=['#F5F5F5','#000000'])
     )
).properties(
    width=300,
    height=300
)

st.altair_chart(chart2)
```

Figure 4-2 shows the resulting graph.

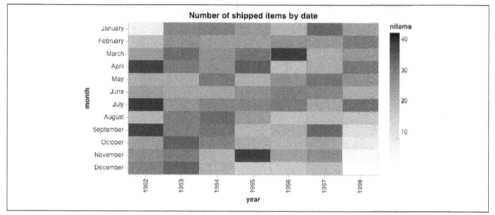

Figure 4-2. A calendar heatmap of number of shipped items

Conclusion

In this chapter, you learned how to deploy a Presto client using different languages, including REST API, Python, R, JDBC, and Node.js. The procedure is the same in all cases: build the Docker image, wrap it into a Kubernetes node, and execute the node to run queries to Presto.

You also implemented a client web service to Presto, showing a simple summary report. The web service queried the TPC-H catalog made available by Presto and showed some statistics related to the number of items by ship date.

In Chapter 5, you'll learn how to perform open data lakehouse analytics.

Open Data Lakehouse Analytics

So far, you have learned how to connect Presto to a data lake using standard connectors such as MySQL and Pinot. In addition, you have learned how to write a custom connector using Presto's Java classes and methods. Finally, you have connected a client to Presto to run generic or custom queries. Now it's time to use Presto in an advanced, more realistic scenario that addresses the main challenges of big data management: table lookup, concurrent access to data, and access control.

In this chapter, we will give an overview of the data lakehouse and implement a practical scenario. The chapter is divided into two parts. In the first part, we introduce the architecture of a data lakehouse, focusing on its main components. In the second part of the chapter, you will implement a practical data lakehouse scenario using Presto and completely open components.

The Emergence of the Lakehouse

The first generation of data lakes, based primarily on the Hadoop Distributed File System (HDFS), demonstrated the promise of analytics at scale. As a result, many organizations formed data platform architectures consisting of data lakes and data warehouses, stitching pipelines and workflows between them. However, the resulting platform was very complex, with issues around reliability, data freshness, and cost.[1]

To overcome these issues, organizations tried to stretch both the data lake and the data warehouse in terms of the workloads they could support, but with limited success.

---

[1] Michael Armbrust, Ali Ghodsi, Reynold Xin, and Matei Zharia, "Lakehouse: a new generation of open platforms that unify data warehousing and advanced analytics," Proceedings of CIDR (2021), *https://oreil.ly/ XFrC_*.

On the data lake side, while systems like Presto significantly improved performance, more sophisticated pipelines and workflows, such as multiple writers or failed executions, required tremendous complexity to handle or led to unreliable results (e.g., corrupted or stale files). On the data warehousing side, there were attempts to bring more data science and machine learning (ML) workloads to these systems, such as Snowflake for AI and ML (*https://oreil.ly/4_Kv-*) and ML in Amazon Redshift (*https://oreil.ly/K1GY8*). However, even with these advances, machine learning—specifically model training—on data warehouses is not a natural fit, and the leading frameworks for model development still rely on direct file access.

Data lakes were introduced in the late 2000s. Since then, we've seen tremendous advances in cloud computing, distributed systems, and artificial intelligence.[2,3] These trends power use cases that ensure the data lake is here to stay. Innovators have continued to look for ways to improve the data management capabilities inside the data lake. In the mid-2010s, a handful of technologies rose to augment the files in a data lake with additional metadata and protocols to bring data management capabilities, such as ACID transactions, efficient updates, and versioning, to the data lake.

In 2020 and early 2021, Michael Armbrust and the colleagues at Databricks introduced and coined the term *lakehouse* as a unified data management system on top of the data lake to combine the benefits of both a data warehouse and a data lake, enabling both traditional data warehousing workloads (i.e., SQL) and advanced analytics (e.g., data science, machine learning, and artificial intelligence). Several years later, the lakehouse is a bona fide system for data storage, management, and processing.[4]

Data Lakehouse Architecture

Figure 5-1 shows the architecture of a data lakehouse composed of these main components: a *data lake*, which includes *table format*, *file format*, and *file store*; a *data science and machine learning* layer; an *SQL query engine*; a *metadata management* layer; and a *data governance* layer. The data lakehouse ingests the data extracted from operational sources, such as structured, semi-structured, and unstructured data, and provides it to analytics applications, such as reporting, dashboarding, workspaces, and applications.

---

2 Alex Krizhevsky, Ilya Sutskever, and Geoffrey E. Hinton, "mageNet classification with deep convolutional neural networks," *NIPS'12: Proceedings of the 25th International Conference on Neural Information Processing Systems* 1 (December 2012): 1097-1105.

3 Ashish Vaswani, Noam Shazeer, Niki Parmar, Jakob Uszkoreit, Llion Jones, Aidan N. Gomez, Łukasz Kaiser, and Illia Polosukhin, "Attention is all you need," *NIPS'17: Proceedings of the 31st International Conference on Neural Information Processing Systems* (December 2017): 6000-6010.

4 Matt Bornstein, Jennifer Li, and Martin Casado, "Emerging Architectures of Modern Data Infrastructure," *Andreessen-Horowitz*, 2020, *https://oreil.ly/Lc6Sv*.

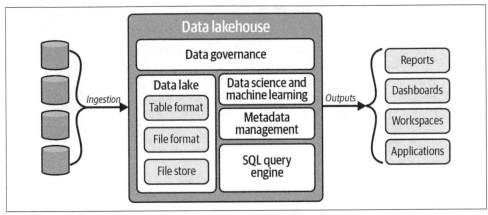

Figure 5-1. The data lakehouse architecture

As this book focuses on Presto, which is designed for SQL workloads, we will be focusing on the SQL lakehouse, which does not include the components for data science and machine learning workloads. Simplistically, we can segment the SQL lakehouse architecture into four distinct components: the *data lake*; the *query engine*; a *metadata management* layer, which helps the query engine to access data quickly; and a *data governance* layer, which ensures data quality in terms of availability, usability, and consistency. The rest of this chapter will focus on understanding each of these individual components, what they do, and how they interact with each other.

Data Lake

As discussed in Chapter 1, the data lake is where enterprises store all their data. The data lake is also a critical component of the SQL lakehouse architecture. The data lake consists of the file store, file format, and table format. A data lake must be relatively cheap to store data and allow any application to utilize a basic API to read and write files as a stream of bytes.

File Store

The file store represents the service where all of the data is stored. The file store is agnostic to the types of data stored on it. Instead, it sees files as collections of bytes. Generally, these file stores fall into categories of filesystems (such as HDFS) or object stores. Amazon Simple Storage Service (S3), Google Cloud Storage, and Azure Blob Storage are the most popular object stores. In this chapter, we will use MinIO (*https://min.io*) as an object store because you can install it locally and because it does not require additional costs, as do the most popular object stores.

Object Stores Versus Filesystems

An *object store* is a type of file store that stores data in a key–value flat structure without a hierarchical filesystem. This flat structure makes it easy to store, retrieve, query, and update data. Object stores differ from filesystems because they do not have a fixed structure or schema. Object stores store data in any format, and you can change the structure of the data at any time. An object store can also store files, allowing only the following operations: PUT, GET, DELETE, and LIST.

The file stores handle and store massive amounts of data. Depending on the deployment, the scale can range from terabytes to exabytes for a single lakehouse deployment. Given the enormous scale of data, the file store is cost-effective.

File Format

In addition to simply storing blobs of bytes, most files stored in the data lake are in a common open format, usually optimized for data access. Parquet and ORC are the most common modern lakehouse file formats. Both are columnar-based storage formats that can more efficiently store data with two key features.

First, they store metadata indexes within the file alongside the data. Thus, processing engines can quickly determine if the data required for a query exists without scanning all the data.

Second, they are columnar-based storage, which means all of the data for a particular column is stored close together in the file. Generally, in SQL engines, columns will all contain data of the same type. This allows the files to achieve higher compression ratios and more efficient space utilization within the data lake.

Table Format

While storing data in file formats, such as Parquet or ORC, is great for the data itself, having only a single set of files to represent a single table can be limiting. In brief, you must also store additional metadata about a table's structure, evolution, and history with the data files. This additional metadata and the protocol surrounding it is called a *table format*.

Table formats introduce another metadata layer on top of file formats to provide a richer abstraction for tables, allowing for performant, advanced data management capabilities, such as ACID transactions, data versioning (i.e., time travel), schema evolution, and efficient IUD (i.e., inserts, upserts, and deletes). This additional metadata layer also allows for lower-level file optimizations, such as file size right-sizing (e.g., larger files are more optimal for analytics) and clustering (e.g., optimizing data colocation).

In practice, table formats consist of additional protocols and metadata stored in the data lake. You could adopt other approaches that implement the table format metadata layer, but this topic is beyond the scope of this book. Widely adopted table formats augment data files in the data lake (e.g., Parquet) with additional metadata files.

All existing table formats add a log level that records all the insert/update operations on the original object stores. Figure 5-2 shows how the table format is organized in an object store. The various table formats differ from each other in how they manage the log level.

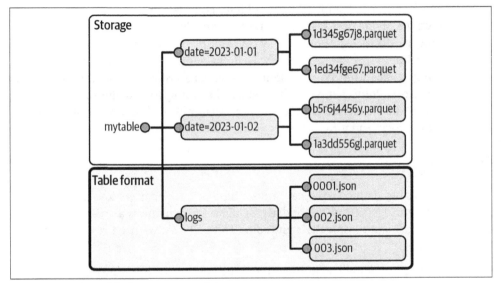

Figure 5-2. The table format in an object store

Today's major table formats are Apache Hudi, Apache Iceberg, and Delta Lake. All are open source and have a primary commercial entity behind them. The most common functionality, such as ACID transitions and data versioning, is virtually identical across all these formats. So naturally, each table format has a slightly different design, given the different focus areas.

Apache Hudi
Uber introduced Hudi to bring data warehousing transactional functionalities to the data lake. Hudi provides an open source utility, named *Hudi DeltaStreamer*, to ingest data from popular sources, such as an SQL database in the Hudi format. Presto supports the Hudi connector. At the time of writing this book, the Hudi connector supports only reading operations. Refer to the Presto documentation (*https://oreil.ly/c6wbR*) for more details.

Apache Iceberg

> Netflix created Apache Iceberg, and one of its original project goals was to scale very large tables in S3-compatible object stores. It could quickly provide results from directory listings of petabyte-scale datasets. Currently, Iceberg doesn't provide any utility to ingest data from popular sources, such as an SQL database, with minimal coding effort. Presto supports the Iceberg connector, which provides both reading and writing capabilities. Refer to the Presto documentation (*https://oreil.ly/areMs*) for more details.

Delta Lake

> Databricks created Delta Lake (now a Linux Foundation project) to enable ACID transactions on the data lakehouse. Delta Lake allows an object store to add new data and read that data consistently, so multiple users reading data will get the same version of that data. Currently, Delta Lake provides only a proprietary utility to ingest data from popular sources, such as an SQL database, with minimal coding effort. Presto supports the Delta Lake connector. At the time of writing this book, the Delta Lake connector supports only reading operations. Refer to the Presto documentation (*https://oreil.ly/F2XIB*) for more details.

Query Engine

The query engines do the analytical processing that enables users and other applications to derive insights from the underlying data. This engine is a critical computing layer from a cost and complexity standpoint. In this book, we use Presto as the main query engine.

SQL query engines in the lakehouse are unique compared to traditional warehouses because the data storage component is entirely separate from the compute component. This separation of responsibilities enables scaling computing capacity separately from storage capacity, potentially resulting in cost savings and additional flexibility for users when compared to traditional warehouses.

Metadata Management

We refer to metadata management as including the technical metadata required for compute engines to properly access and manage (e.g., update) the underlying data lake files. Metadata management does not include metadata related to data governance, such as metadata for data access control.

Usually, a data lake ingests data derived from different sources. A data lake uses a metadata catalog to keep track of the data stored within it and for data discovery (table lookup). Metadata is essential for understanding what data is available, where it is located, and how a data lake can access it.

The Hive Metastore (HMS) is one of the most popular metadata catalogs. HMS provides centralized storage for Hive tables and partition metadata. Clients access it via the metastore service API. Presto supports the Hive connector. Refer to the Presto documentation (*https://oreil.ly/0xoyW*) for more details.

Figure 5-3 shows how Presto performs table lookup using a metadata catalog. First, the Presto client runs a query using the table `transactions` contained in the `glue` catalog under the schema `pq`. Upon receiving the query, Presto asks the metadata catalog for the location of the `transactions` table. The metadata returns to Presto the complete path to the `transactions` table. Next, Presto runs the query and returns the results to the Presto client. A metadata catalog contains more than just file locations. It can also include other helpful metadata for optimizing queries, such as information about the table (table name, column names, and column types), indexing, and views.

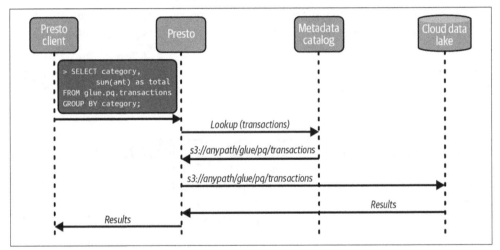

Figure 5-3. How the metadata catalog works

Data Governance

A lakehouse incorporates a data governance layer. Data governance refers to managing, controlling, and protecting an organization's data assets to ensure data quality, integrity, privacy, and compliance with relevant regulations and policies. Examples of data governance areas include:

Access control
Who can access data at what level (e.g., read-only, specific tables, columns, or rows)?

Discovery
How do individuals discover data?

Semantic definition
What does particular data mean, particularly in a domain or business?

Data lineage
How was this data created, and can you trace its heritage?

Data observability
Understanding the health and quality of your data.

Covering all these areas of data governance would take a book on its own. So instead, we will focus on access control.

Data Access Control

Data access control is a security measure that protects data in a data lakehouse by restricting access only to authorized users. Organizations prevent unauthorized access and misuse of sensitive or confidential information by controlling who can access the data and what they can do with it.

Administrators can grant users different levels of data access control by setting the fine-grained permissions described in Table 5-1.

Table 5-1. Fine-grained permissions by access control level

Access control level	Permissions
Database	Users can modify the whole database by creating, deleting, and updating tables.
Table	Users can modify the whole database by creating, deleting, and updating tables.
Column	Users can read and modify only some columns in a table.
Row	Users can read and modify only some rows in a table.

Figure 5-4 shows an example of different levels of data access control. At the database security level, the user can access only database A. At the table security level, they can access only table C. At the column security level, users can access only columns E and F. Finally, at the row security level, they can access only rows G and H.

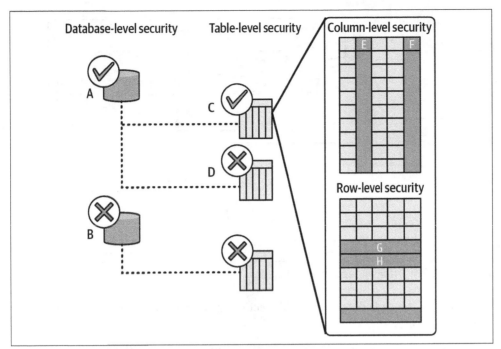

Figure 5-4. Different levels of data access control

Building a Data Lakehouse

In Chapter 1 we introduced our case study, focusing on connecting Presto to a data lake. Now it's time to expand on the scenario described in Figure 1-7 by incorporating Presto into a data lakehouse.

Figure 5-5 shows the architecture of the scenario we'll implement in this section. The figure highlights the main components in dark gray and the auxiliary components in light gray. As an object store, we'll use MinIO to store the data using the Hudi table format. To initialize the MinIO store, we'll implement a MinIO client, and to write data in the MinIO store, we'll implement a data stream in Spark. We won't use Presto directly because, at present, it does not support writing operations in the Hudi format. Then, we'll connect Presto to a Hive Metastore to retrieve the data from the MinIO store. The Hive Metastore will use a MySQL database as an internal storage. Finally, we'll attach a Presto client to Presto to get data from the MinIO store. We'll implement each component as a separate pod of the Kubernetes cluster you have already implemented in Chapter 2.

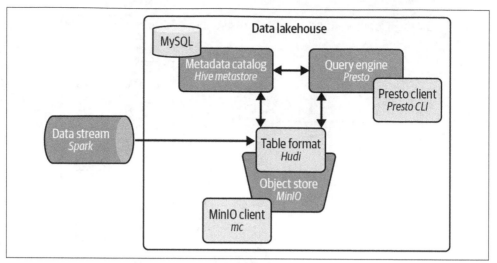

Figure 5-5. The implemented scenario

You can find the code described in this section in the book's GitHub repository under the directory *05/*.

We'll implement the scenario by running the following incremental steps:

1. Configuring MinIO

2. Configuring HMS

3. Configuring Spark

4. Registering Hudi tables with HMS

5. Connecting and querying Presto

Configuring MinIO

Refer to *05/data_lakehouse/minio.yaml* to configure MinIO. Implement the MinIO container as a `ReplicationController` using the *quay.io/minio/minio:RELEASE.2022-06-17T02-00-35Z* image available on Docker Hub. Then, start the storage service with the `minio server /data --console-address :9090` command.

Add this command to the container specs in the *minio.yaml* file:

```
spec:
  containers:
   - name: minio
     image:  quay.io/minio/minio:latest
     command:
```

```
- /bin/bash
- -c
args:
- minio server /data --console-address :9090
```

MinIO requires a username and a password for access, so set them up using the two environment variables MINIO_ROOT_USER and MINIO_ROOT_PASSWORD that the MinIO Docker image requires:

```
env:
- name: MINIO_ROOT_USER
  valueFrom:
    secretKeyRef:
      key: minio_root_user
      name: minio-secrets
- name: MINIO_ROOT_PASSWORD
  valueFrom:
    secretKeyRef:
      key: minio_root_password
      name: minio-secrets
```

Store the MinIO secrets as a separate component of the Kubernetes cluster, named minio-secrets. Find the implementation of this component in the *minio-secrets.yaml* file.

MinIO accepts new connections from the 9000 port, so add a service to the *minio.yaml* file that listens to both ports, 9090 for console and 9000 for new connections:

```
apiVersion: v1
kind: Service
metadata:
  name: minio
spec:
  ports:
    - name: minio-console
      port: 9090
      targetPort: 9090
    - name: minio-api
      port: 9000
      targetPort: 9000
  type: LoadBalancer
  selector:
    app: minio
```

To deploy the MinIO object store, run the following commands:

```
kubectl create -f minio-secrets.yaml --namespace presto
kubectl apply -f minio.yaml --namespace presto
```

Point to *http://localhost:9090/* in your browser to access the MinIO web interface. Use the credentials stored in `minio-secrets` to log in. The storage does not contain any buckets.

Populating MinIO

Use a MinIO client (`mc` in this example) to define the initial structure of the storage. We'll create two buckets: `warehouse`, which will contain raw data, and `metastore`, which will include data in the Hudi format. Also, we'll add a sample table, named *customers.csv*, to *warehouse/data*.

Table 5-2 shows a snapshot of the `customers` table.

Table 5-2. A snapshot of the customers table

id	first	last	gender	dob	zip	city	state
6895	Valerie	Whitney	F	1959-03-31	99160	Orient	WA
4509	Crystal	Smith	F	1974-01-03	96135	Vinton	CA
8045	Christine	Maxwell	F	1985-08-21	91321	Newhall	CA
8593	Sharon	Mclaughlin	F	1954-07-05	94015	Daly City	CA

The table is not stored in the Hudi format yet. We'll use Spark to convert the table to a Hudi table and store it in the `metastore` branch.

Deploy the MinIO client as a separate pod in the Kubernetes cluster. Refer to *05/data_lakehouse/mc.yaml* to configure the MinIO client.

Implement the MinIO client container as a `ReplicationController` using the *minio/mc* image available on Docker Hub.

Use the *minio/mc* image available in Docker Hub and configure the `sleep infinity` command to keep the pod alive:

```
containers:
  - name: mc
    image: minio/mc
    command: [ "sleep" ]
    args: [ "infinity" ]
```

Read the `MINIO_USERNAME` and `MINIO_PASSWORD` environment variables from `minio-secrets` to access the MinIO storage:

```
env:
 - name: MINIO_USERNAME
   valueFrom:
     secretKeyRef:
       key: minio_root_user
       name: minio-secrets
 - name: MINIO_PASSWORD
   valueFrom:
     secretKeyRef:
       key: minio_root_password
       name: minio-secrets
```

Finally, mount the */data* directory containing the sample tables as an external directory in the host filesystem:

```
containers:
 - name: mc
   # other specs
   mountPath: "/data/"

volumes:
 - name: data
   hostPath:
     path: "/absolute/path/to/data/storage"
```

To deploy the MinIO object store, run the following command:

```
kubectl apply -f mc.yaml --namespace presto
```

Then, enter the MinIO client container and create two buckets, warehouse for the raw data and metastore for HMS:

```
/usr/bin/mc config host add minio http://minio:9000\
${MINIO_USERNAME} ${MINIO_PASSWORD}
/usr/bin/mc mb minio/warehouse;
/usr/bin/mc mb minio/metastore;
```

Finally, populate the warehouse bucket with the content of the *data* directory:

```
/usr/bin/mc cp --recursive /data minio/warehouse;
```

Access the MinIO web interface again. You should see two buckets: metastore, which is empty, and warehouse, which contains *data/customers.csv*, as shown in Figure 5-6.

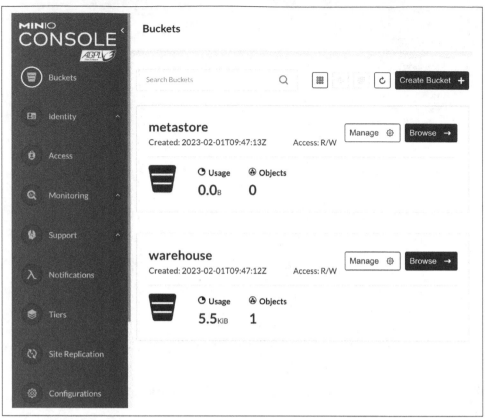

Figure 5-6. The two buckets in MinIO after running the MinIO client

Configuring HMS

We'll use HMS as an intermediary between the MinIO store and Presto. In our configuration, HMS will access only the `metastore` bucket of the MinIO store, where we will insert the Hudi tables.

To configure HMS, start by creating the MySQL node that HMS will use to store data. Refer to *05/data_lakehouse/mysq-metastore.yaml*.

```
kubectl apply -f mysql-metastore.yaml --namespace presto
```

Next, configure the *05/dockerfiles/hive-metastore/conf/hive-site.xml* file with the following information:

- The MinIo endpoint:

```xml
<property>
    <name>fs.s3a.endpoint</name>
    <value>http://minio:9000</value>
</property>
```

- The MinIO credentials, `jdo.option.ConnectionUserName` and `javax.jdo` `.option.ConnectionPassword`:

```xml
<property>
    <name>javax.jdo.option.ConnectionUserName</name>
    <value>admin</value>
</property>
<property>
    <name>javax.jdo.option.ConnectionPassword</name>
    <value>admin</value>
</property>
```

- The metastore warehouse directory. Set it to *s3a://metastore/warehouse/*.

- The MySQL configuration parameters:

```xml
<property>
    <name>javax.jdo.option.ConnectionDriverName</name>
    <value>com.mysql.cj.jdbc.Driver</value>
</property>

<property>
    <name>javax.jdo.option.ConnectionURL</name>
    <value>jdbc:mysql://mysql-metastore:3306/metastore_db?
    createDatabaseIfNotExist=true</value>
</property>
```

Then, build the Spark Docker image, contained in the *05/dockerfiles/hive-metastore* directory:

```
docker build -t hive-metastore .
```

Finally, use *05/data_lakehouse/hive-metastore.yaml* to create the HMS node in the Kubernetes cluster:

```
kubectl apply -f hive-metastore.yaml --namespace presto
```

Figure 5-7 shows how we'll organize the MinIO store. There are two buckets: `ware house` for raw data and `metastore` for Hudi tables.

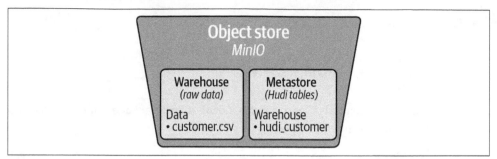

Figure 5-7. How we will organize the MinIO store

Configuring Spark

We'll use Spark to convert the raw *customer.csv* table contained in the *warehouse/data* bucket to the hudi_customer table contained in the *metastore/warehouse* bucket.

Start by building the Spark Docker image, contained in the *05/dockerfiles/spark* directory:

```
docker build -t spark .
```

Then, create the Kubernetes pod referring to the *spark.yaml* file contained in the *05/data_lakehouse* directory:

```
kubectl apply -f spark.yaml --namespace presto
```

Figure 5-8 resumes the lakehouse scenario implemented so far. You have deployed three main components (MinIO, HMS, and Spark) as well as two auxiliary components: MySQL metastore and MinIO client.

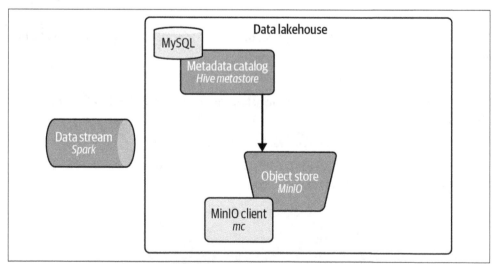

Figure 5-8. A snapshot of the data lakehouse components implemented so far

Registering Hudi Tables with HMS

So far, the MinIO object store contains just one table, named *customers.csv*, under the *warehouse/data* path. We will use Spark to convert the CSV table into a Hudi table.

Enter the Spark container and launch the Spark shell with the MinIO and HMS configurations:

```
spark-shell \
--packages org.apache.hadoop:hadoop-aws:3.3.1, \
org.apache.hudi:hudi-spark3.2-bundle_2.12:0.11.1 \
--conf spark.hadoop.fs.s3a.access.key="dbuser" \
--conf spark.hadoop.fs.s3a.secret.key="minio123" \
--conf spark.hadoop.fs.s3a.endpoint=http://minio:9000 \
--conf spark.hadoop.fs.s3a.path.style.access=true \
--conf spark.hadoop.hive.metastore.uris=\
"thrift://hive-metastore:9083" \
--conf spark.sql.warehouse.dir="s3a://metastore/" \
--conf spark.sql.catalog.spark_catalog.type=hive \
--conf spark.sql.catalog.spark_catalog.uri=thrift://hive-metastore:9083 \
--conf spark.sql.catalog.spark_catalog.warehouse=s3a://metastore/ \
--conf spark.sql.catalog.spark_catalog\
=org.apache.spark.sql.hudi.catalog.HoodieCatalog \
--conf spark.sql.extensions\
=org.apache.spark.sql.hudi.HoodieSparkSessionExtension \
--conf spark.serializer=org.apache.spark.serializer.KryoSerializer \
"${@-}"
```

In the Spark shell, we use Scala as a programming language. Refer to *05/data_lakehouse/scripts/hudi-customers-create.scala* for more details.

In the Spark shell, first import the required libraries:

```
import org.apache.hudi.QuickstartUtils._
import scala.collection.JavaConversions._
import org.apache.spark.sql.SaveMode._
import org.apache.hudi.DataSourceReadOptions._
import org.apache.hudi.DataSourceWriteOptions._
import org.apache.hudi.config.HoodieWriteConfig._
import org.apache.spark.sql.functions.monotonicallyIncreasingId
```

Next, load the *customers.csv* table from the *warehouse/data* bucket:

```
val df = spark.read.options(Map("header" -> "true")
).csv("s3a://warehouse/data/customers.csv")
```

Then, add the uuid column to the dataset as required by HMS:

```
val df2 = df.withColumn("uuid", monotonicallyIncreasingId)
```

Finally, save the table to MinIO as a Hudi table:

```
df2.write.format("hudi").
    options(getQuickstartWriteConfigs).
    option(RECORDKEY_FIELD_OPT_KEY, "id").
    option(PRECOMBINE_FIELD_OPT_KEY, "dob").
    option(TABLE_NAME, tableName).
    mode(Overwrite).
    saveAsTable("hudi_customers")
```

Access the MinIO web interface and open the *metastore/warehouse* bucket. You should see the Hudi version of the customer table, as shown in Figure 5-9.

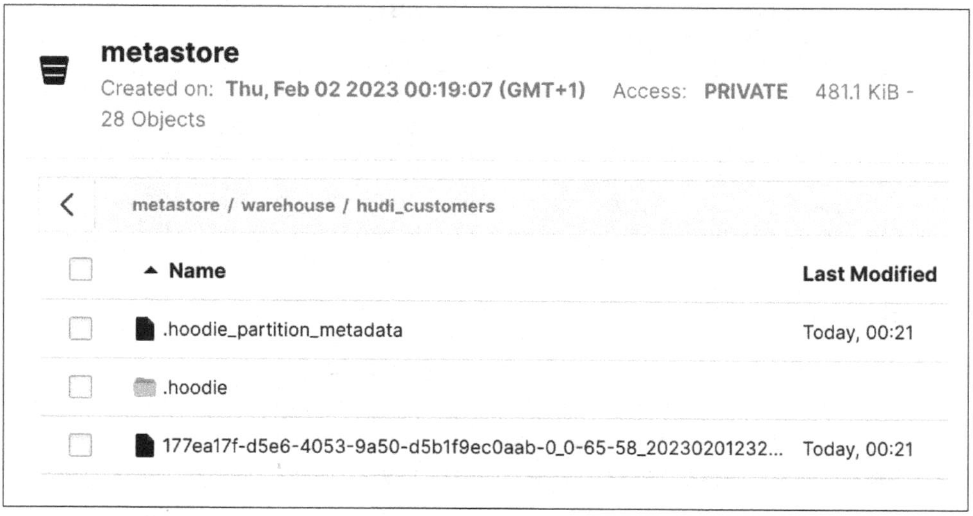

Figure 5-9. The customer Hudi table in the MinIO store

Connecting and Querying Presto

We'll connect Presto to HMS to query the hudi_customer table. Since version 0.275, Presto supports Hudi natively, so we can configure a Hudi connector directly. As a Presto instance, we'll use the Presto sandbox (*https://oreil.ly/eeJEz*). Refer to *05/data_lakehouse/presto-coordinator.yaml* to configure the Presto coordinator. Prepare a directory with all the Presto configuration files (*05/data_lakehouse/conf*) and mount it in the Presto instance. Use the Hudi connector to read Hudi tables in Presto. The Hudi connector requires the following parameters:

```
connector.name=hudi
hive.metastore.uri=thrift://hive-metastore:9083
```

In addition to the connector name, specify the MinIO endpoint (hive.s3.endpoint) and a compatible S3 store (hive.s3.path-style-access=true).

The Presto sandbox requires the MinIO credentials as environment variables. Set them in the *presto-coordinator.yaml* file:

```
spec:
    containers:
        ...
        env:
        - name: AWS_ACCESS_KEY_ID
          valueFrom:
            secretKeyRef:
              key: minio_root_user
              name: minio-secrets
        - name: AWS_SECRET_ACCESS_KEY
          valueFrom:
            secretKeyRef:
              key: minio_root_password
              name: minio-secrets
```

If you don't have enough resources in your local machine to run a complete Presto cluster, instantiate only the Presto coordinator. After deploying the Presto coordinator, deploy a Presto client, as described in Chapter 4. In this section, we'll use the Presto CLI, available in the Presto coordinator.

Log in to the Presto coordinator and launch the Presto CLI, using the `presto-cli` command:

```
sh-4.2# presto-cli
```

Note that in the previous chapters we used the `presto` command to run the Presto CLI. Here, the command is different because we are using another Docker image to run Presto:

Then, set the database to query as follows (`hudi.default`):

```
presto> use hudi.default;
USE
```

List the available tables in the database:

```
presto:default> show tables;
    Table
----------------
 hudi_customers
(1 row)

Query 20230202_115014_00002_xpzub, FINISHED, 1 node
Splits: 19 total, 19 done (100.00%)
0:14 [2 rows, 60B] [0 rows/s, 4B/s]
```

Finally, run the following query to the Hudi table:

```
presto:default> SELECT last,gender,dob,zip,city,state
FROM hudi_customers
WHERE first = 'Sharon';
   last    | gender |    dob     |  zip  |   city      | state
-----------+--------+------------+-------+-------------+-------
 Mclaughlin | F     | 1954-07-05 | 94015 | Daly City   | CA
 Ayala      | F     | 1956-09-01 | 94619 | Oakland     | CA
 Harper     | F     | 1978-06-21 | 95827 | Sacramento  | CA
 Clark      | F     | 1976-09-17 | 99160 | Orient      | WA
(4 rows)

Query 20230203_062422_00005_93snn, FINISHED, 1 node
Splits: 17 total, 17 done (100.00%)
0:06 [86 rows, 427KB] [15 rows/s, 75.9KB/s]
```

The result of the query demonstrates that the data lakehouse is perfectly set up and working.

Conclusion

In this chapter, you reviewed the essential components of a data lakehouse, including data lake storage, data lake table formats, the query engine, the metadata catalog, and data access control, as a specific case of data governance. The data lake storage enables you to store data in the object store format, which is more efficient for big data. MinIO and Amazon S3 are examples of data lake storage. The data lake table format enables you to manage transactions and similar operations when you access data, thus keeping data consistency and, in general, all the ACID operations. The Hudi format is an example of a data lake table format. The query engine provides a single point to access many catalogs within a data lakehouse. Presto is an example of a query engine. The metadata catalog provides the data lake with efficient table lookup and data discovery. HMS is an example of table lookup. Finally, access control provides all the rules to define who can access data, even at a fine-grained level.

In the second part of the chapter, you implemented a data lakehouse scenario with Presto, MinIO, HMS, Spark, and Hudi. First, you transformed a simple table available as a CSV file into a Hudi table. Then you stored it in the HMS metastore and accessed it through Presto.

In Chapter 6, you'll learn how to perform Presto administration.

Presto Administration

Presto administration is the set of tools, behaviors, and strategies that enable you to maintain your Presto cluster. The flow to administer Presto comprises three steps: configuration, monitoring, and management. Configuration defines how to set up your Presto cluster before deploying it. Monitoring enables you to control the behavior of your Presto cluster while it is deployed. Finally, management permits you to adapt the behavior of your Presto cluster to the runtime conditions.

The chapter is organized into three parts. In the first part, you'll learn how to configure Presto through the configuration file, session properties, and the Java Virtual Machine (JVM). In the second part, you'll learn Presto's tools to monitor the Presto cluster: Presto console, REST API, and evaluation metrics. In the third part, you'll learn how to manage Presto, with a focus on resources, sessions, and namespaces.

Introducing Presto Administration

Administration in Presto refers to the tasks and responsibilities involved in configuring, managing, and maintaining a Presto deployment.

As a database administrator, your role will be to ensure that the Presto system operates efficiently and effectively and handles the workload of running complex queries on large datasets. Administration may involve monitoring the system's performance, optimizing configuration parameters, and managing the data stored in the system.

Figure 6-1 shows the steps involved in the Presto administration. See the steps as a continuous loop. Configuration is the initial setup of the loop, which includes specifying the initial Presto running conditions. Monitoring is ongoing to check that the conditions remain met. Management is responsible for making necessary changes to the Presto configuration, such as adjusting the conditions or changing the actions.

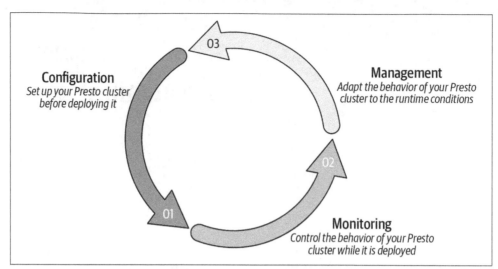

Figure 6-1. The steps involved in Presto administration

Configuration

When working with Presto in production or during development, ensure that the Presto configuration is set up correctly. Presto supports three types of configurations: properties, sessions, and JVM.

Properties

Presto has hundreds of configuration properties for tuning the service for optimal performance. Typically you set these properties based on the available resources of the host node. When configuring a production cluster, run dedicated nodes (instances) and don't share the instances with applications other than the host OS and lightweight monitoring software. In the case of VMs and bare-metal instances, this means one Presto process per node. For Kubernetes, this typically indicates a single container per node to avoid noisy neighbors.

In Presto, in the *config.properties* file you can configure the following common categories of properties that you will use when getting started:

General

This is a set of generic properties, such the `join-distribution-type` and `redistribute-writes` properties. The `join-distribution-type` property enables you to specify the type of distributed join to use. Allowed values are `AUTOMATIC`, `PARTITIONED`, and `BROADCAST`. The `redistribute-writes` specifies whether to redistribute data before writing. Allowed values are `TRUE` and `FALSE`.

Memory management

This is a set of properties that specify how much memory a query can use. Usually, memory management properties start with the keyword `query`. There are two types of memory allocation: *user memory* and *system memory*. The user memory includes query aggregation and sorting operations. The system memory includes read, write, table scans, and similar functions. Examples of memory management properties include `query.max-memory` and `query.max-total-memory-per-node`.

Spilling

Spilling is the process of moving memory to disk. Enable spilling if you want to run large queries that do not fit memory. The cost to pay is a slower query. To enable spilling, set `experimental.spill-enabled` to `true`. For the other spilling configuration properties, refer to the Presto documentation (*https://oreil.ly/4Eohl*). Spilling properties are still experimental at the time of writing and start with the keyword `experimental`.

Exchange

This is a set of properties that specify how Presto nodes must transfer data to each other. Usually, exchange properties start with the keyword `exchange`. Examples of exchange properties include `exchange.max-buffer-size` and `exchange.max-response-size`.

Task

A task is any work assigned by the coordinator to a worker. Use the task properties to adjust the workers' workload. Task properties start with the keyword `task`. Examples of task properties are `task.max-worker-threads` and `task.concurrency`.

Node scheduler

The Presto scheduler splits a query plan into smaller units of logical works, called *splits*. Use the node scheduler properties to manage splits. These properties start with the keyword `node-scheduler`. Examples of node schedule properties include `node-scheduler.max-splits-per-node` and `node-scheduler.include-coordinator`.

Optimizer

This is a set of properties to optimize some queries, such as joins, aggregations, parallelism, etc. These properties start with the keyword `optimizer`. Examples of optimizer properties are `optimizer.optimize-metadata-queries` and `optimizer.push-aggregation-through-join`.

Planner

> This is a set of properties to configure how Presto must manage query planning. These properties start with the keyword `planner`. An example of planner properties is `planner.query-analyzer-timeout`.

Regular expression functions

> This is a set of properties to tune the regular expression functions in a query. Presto supports two libraries for regular expression: `JONI` and `RE2J`. Use the `regex-library` to specify which library to use. Then, depending on the chosen library, configure the associated properties.

How to configure a cluster

The million-dollar question that often gets asked is, "How do I choose the size and configuration of the cluster?" As always, the answer is, "It depends." Every workload is different—it depends on concurrency, query types (simple, aggregations, memory intensive, or compute intensive), and data size. In general, our recommendation is to start with a *reasonable cluster size*.

A good place to start is to use r5 (memory optimized) instance types on AWS (or the corresponding ones on other cloud providers). Table 6-1 shows the suggested node types on AWS and the number of nodes based on the workload size, as explained in the blog post "Five workload characteristics to consider when right sizing Amazon ElastiCache Redis clusters" (*https://oreil.ly/xKLac*).

Table 6-1. Suggested node types on AWS and number of nodes based on the workload size

Workload	Transactions per second (TPS)	Data size	Node type on AWS	Number of nodes
Small	< 2,000	< 10 GB	r5.8xlarge	5–10
Medium	Between 2,000 and 20,000	Between 20,000 GB and 100 GB	r5.4xlarge	20–40
Large	> 20,000	> 100 GB	r5.16xlarge	50+

Run your representative queries with the right concurrency, and benchmark the performance results under various configurations. You can then tweak the cluster up and down from there. There isn't a one-size-fits-all. Often your workloads will change, and you will need to either set up a new cluster for the new workload or add capacity to the cluster (managed via resource groups) to make the queries run efficiently on the cluster.

Sessions

In parity with modern databases, Presto enables you to partially configure the behavior of its underlying engine using session properties. However, you can configure only a subset of all available properties using session properties. For the other properties, edit the *config.properties* or *node.properties* file.

Typically, Presto hyphenates configuration properties with the - symbol, and session properties with the _ symbol. For example, `join-distribution-type` is a configuration property, and `join_distribution_type` is its related session property.

To list all the session properties, log in to your Presto client and run the following command:

```
presto> SHOW SESSION;
```

As an output, Presto shows a long list of properties similar to the following:

```
                 Name                          |         Value
-----------------------------------------------+------------------------
 aggregation_if_to_filter_rewrite_strategy     | DISABLED
 aggregation_operator_unspill_memory_limit     | 4MB
 aggregation_partitioning_merging_strategy     | LEGACY
 aggregation_spill_enabled                     | true
 allow_window_order_by_literals                | true
 check_access_control_on_utilized_columns_only | false
 check_access_control_with_subfields           | false
 colocated_join                                | true
 ...
```

To change the value of a session property, use the SET SESSION command:

```
SET SESSION <property> = <value>;
```

For example, set `join_distribution_type` to PARTITIONED:

```
SET SESSION join_distribution_type="PARTITIONED";
```

To reset the default value for a session property, use the RESET command:

```
SET SESSION <property>;
RESET SESSION;
```

Using sessions

As an example of how sessions work, run the following experiment:

1. Log in to your Presto client in your Presto coordinator. Then, run the following query:

   ```
   SELECT * FROM tpch.tiny.customer LIMIT 5;
   ```

2. In addition to the query result, the output shows other information, including the number of fetched rows per second (166 rows/s in the example):

```
Query 20221129_085214_00002_i3xsn, FINISHED, 1 node
Splits: 21 total, 21 done (100.00%)
0:09 [1.5K rows, 0B] [166 rows/s, 0B/s]
```

3. Try to optimize the query by enabling the runtime optimizer:

```
SET SESSION join_reordering_strategy='AUTOMATIC';
```

4. Rerun the previous query:

```
SELECT * FROM tpch.tiny.customer LIMIT 5;
```

5. Presto should have increased the number of fetched queries per second (296 rows/s in the example). As a result, the query is faster.

```
Query 20230406_212505_00007_3htmf, FINISHED, 1 node
Splits: 21 total, 21 done (100.00%)
0:05 [1.5K rows, 0B] [296 rows/s, 0B/s]
```

JVM

Officially Presto supports only JDK 8. However, PrestoDB can also use Java 11 JRE for its runtime. This version of Java provides added optimizations and enables more fine-tuning with Java's next-generation garbage collection mechanisms.

Specify the tunable parameters for the Presto JVM in the *jvm.config* file, as we discussed in Chapter 2. Common parameters include memory and garbage collector.

Memory

Typically, set the initial JVM memory to 70% of the machine's available memory (leaving 30% to the OS). However, as the host machine gets larger in terms of memory consumption, and the background services on the OS are limited, the JVM allocates more memory to Presto. Pre-allocating memory to Presto provides two key advantages:

- The memory allocation is not significantly fragmented (contiguous memory pages as much as possible), which results in more efficient JVM operations when cleaning up and marking objects for garbage collection (GC).

- The JVM does not request memory allocations in the middle of query executions, which can result in JVM pauses as it copies different generations of objects and pages to new addresses.

Set the -Xms (minimum JVM memory) and -Xmx (minimum JVM memory) to the same values to pre-allocate a specific value to Presto memory. Putting these parameters at the same value prevents JVM resizing. It is also highly recommended to have parity in node configurations across the cluster, much like any distributed database/engine. Maintaining different configurations on different nodes can lead to unexpected behavior and variance, as the same query may behave differently, depending on the node to which it is assigned.

Out-of-memory errors

To handle out-of-memory errors, set the following parameters:

`-XX:+HeapDumpOnOutOfMemoryError`
  Dump memory into a physical file in case of an out-of-memory error.

`-XX:+ExitOnOutOfMemoryError`
  Run the `exit` command in case of an out-of-memory error.

`-XX:+UseGCOverheadLimit`
  Limit the JVM's time spent in GC before an out-of-memory error is thrown.

Garbage collection

To monitor Presto's health as a process running in the JVM, enable logging of GC activity, as shown in the following JVM configuration:

```
-Xloggc:/opt/presto/log/gc-%t.log
-XX:+PrintGCDetails
-XX:+PrintGCDateStamps
-XX:+PrintGCApplicationConcurrentTime
-XX:+PrintGCApplicationStoppedTime
-XX:+PrintGCCause
-XX:+PrintGCTimeStamps
-XX:+PrintReferenceGC
-XX:+PrintClassHistogramAfterFullGC
-XX:+PrintClassHistogramBeforeFullGC
```

Restart the Presto cluster to make the changes effective. To see GC logs visually, use an online tool, such as GCeasy (*https://gceasy.io*):

1. Download the log file. Open a terminal and run the following command to copy the GC log file from the Docker container to your host:

   ```
   docker cp <container_id>:/opt/presto/log/gc-<date>.log .
   ```

2. Upload the GC log file in GCeasy. Once the upload is complete, GCeasy shows you a GC Intelligence Report, which includes statistics and charts. Figure 6-2 shows the JVM memory size visualization produced by GCeasy. Refer to the GCeasy report for the other generated charts and statistics.

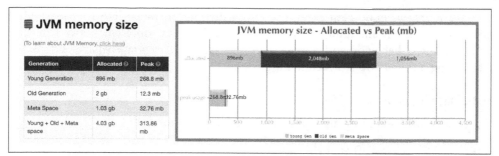

Figure 6-2. The JVM memory size visualization produced by GCeasy

Monitoring

Monitoring a Presto cluster involves keeping track of the health, performance, and resource utilization of the nodes in the cluster. Monitoring helps you identify potential issues or problems with the system and take appropriate action to resolve them.

You can use three tools to monitor your Presto cluster: Presto console, REST API, and JMX metrics.

Console

The Presto console is a web interface that provides details about the cluster and its current health. The web interface is accessible on the Presto coordinator via HTTP or HTTPS, depending upon your setup. The default port for the web interface is 8080, but you can change it in the *config.properties* file by setting `http-server.http.port`. Additionally, you can protect access to the console through an authentication mechanism. We'll describe how to set up authentication in Chapter 7.

Figure 6-3 shows the home page of the Presto console. The home page contains various details about the cluster, such as the version, the environment name, and the uptime (i.e., the time since the coordinator was last restarted). The console also contains summary information about all the types of queries, such as planned, blocked, finished, failed, and so on. Click a single query to access its detailed description.

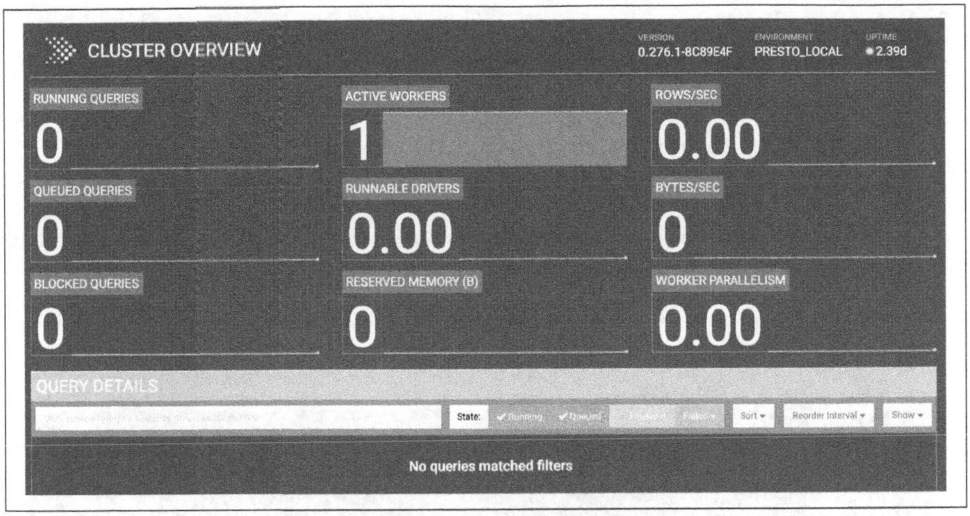

Figure 6-3. An overview of the home page of the Presto console

Detailed information about a query includes:

Session
> Any nondefault configuration overrides or special session property settings set when the user submits the query.

Execution
> Information related to time, such as submission time, completion time, elapsed time, etc.

Resource utilization summary and timeline
> Shows a summary of used resources during the query execution, such as CPU time, scheduled time, blocked time, peak user memory, and so on.

RuntimeStats
> Additional metrics for each stage of the query. A stage is a logical subsegment of a query, as broken down by the coordinator query execution plan.

Query
> Details of each stage of the executed query, the number of resources utilized, and the time taken.

Using the console for monitoring

Consider the following test example:

1. Start your Presto cluster.

2. Enter your Presto coordinator through the command-line terminal, and access the Presto client by typing presto in the terminal.

3. Run the following query:

   SELECT * FROM tpch.tiny.customer LIMIT 5;

4. Point to the following URL in your browser: *http://localhost:8080*.

5. In the QUERY DETAILS box, click Finished. You should see the details related to your last query, as shown in Figure 6-4.

6. Click the query ID (20221126_223520_00008_i3xsn in the example) to access the query details.

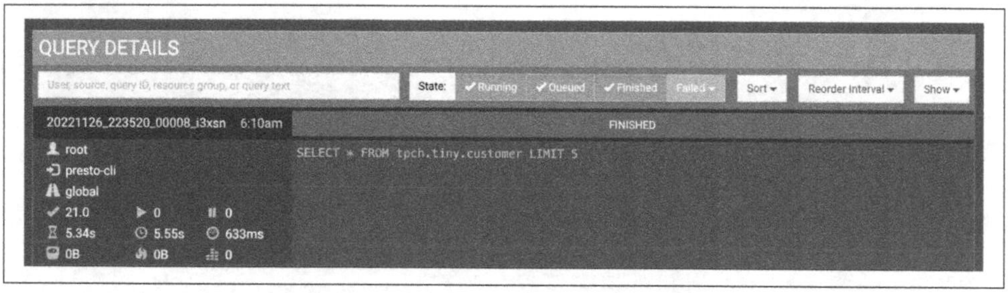

Figure 6-4. Overview of a query in the Presto console

Using the console for debugging

Consider the following query with a syntax error: SELECT * FROM tpch.tiny. customers LIMIT 5;. The customers table doesn't exist in the tiny schema. Run the query in the Presto client. The Presto client returns an error.

Access the error details in your Presto console by clicking Failed in the query details box and then User Error. Next, select the query ID corresponding to your query. In the Error Information box, Presto reports all the details about the error, including the error type, the error code, and the stack trace.

You can also use the Presto console to debug more complex errors.

Using the console for going over the interactive plan

Run the following query in the Presto client: SELECT * FROM tpch.tiny.customer LIMIT 5;. Access the query details in your Presto console by clicking Finished in the query details box and then selecting your query. Click Live Plan to access the query interactive plan (Figure 6-5). We'll see the query execution plan in Chapter 8.

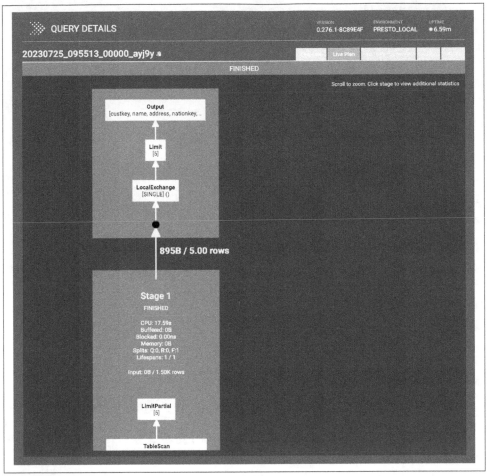

Figure 6-5. An example of a query interactive plan

REST API

Use the REST API to monitor Presto behavior. Here is a short list of some of the available Presto endpoints:

```
/v1/node
/v1/node/failed
/v1/execute
/v1/statement
/v1/query
/v1/query/<query_id>
/v1/thread
/ui/thread
/v1/task
```

```
/v1/task/<task_id>
/v1/jmx/mbean/<object_name>
```

The REST API HTTP methods include:

- A `POST` to `/v1/statement` runs the query string in the POST body and returns a JSON document containing the query results. The JSON document will have a `nextUri` URL attribute if there are more results.
- A `GET` to the `nextUri` attribute returns the next batch of query results.
- A `DELETE` to the `nextUri` terminates a running query.

You have already seen how to implement a REST API-based client in Chapter 4. For example, use the `query` endpoint to get general metrics on the last queries. To obtain information about a specific query, specify the query ID, for example:

```
http://presto-coordinator:8080/v1/query/20211109_165830_00006_zadq6
```

`20211109_165830_00006_zadq6` is the specific query ID of the example.

Metrics

Presto exposes system metrics via JMX MBeans. Access these metrics using the following mechanisms: JMX connector, REST API, and JMX exporters.

JMX connector

Presto provides a JMX (Java Management Extensions) connector catalog to query its own JMX endpoint to fetch metrics using the same SQL syntax. The JMX endpoint is helpful for quickly viewing metrics of queries just run and is a clever way of testing your environment.

To configure the JMX catalog, add the following configuration property to the *presto-config-map.yaml* file:

```
jmx.properties: |
    connector.name=jmx
```

Add a volume mount point and a volume for the JMX connector in the *presto-coordinator.yaml* and *presto-workers.yaml* files, as described in Chapter 2, and restart your Presto cluster.

For example, run the following query in your Presto client to get the free bytes in the standard or reserved memory pool:

```
SELECT
  freebytes, node
FROM
  jmx.current." com.facebook.presto.memory:*type=memorypool*";
```

REST API

Presto provides the following REST API endpoint to access the JMX metrics:

```
http://<coordinator>:<port>/v1/jmx/
```

Unlike the query endpoint, the JMX endpoint doesn't provide results pagination, showing all metrics on the cluster for all queries. To minimize the risk of getting an incredible number of results, select a particular object for which you'd like to observe the metrics and query it.

Refer to the Presto documentation (*https://oreil.ly/FAuEG*) for more information on using a JMX connector.

JMX exporters

JMX is a Java technology that provides a standard way of monitoring and managing Java-based applications. Use the JMX exporters to expose JMX metrics from a Java application to external monitoring systems, such as Prometheus (*https://prometheus.io*) or Grafana (*https://grafana.com*).

In the context of Presto, use JMX exporters to monitor and manage the system and query metrics.

To make Presto work with Prometheus, download the Prometheus JMX exporter JAR file from the Prometheus website (*https://oreil.ly/S_wZC*) and put it in your Presto coordinator node. Then, create a *prometheus.yaml* file containing all the metrics you want to export, and put it in your Presto coordinator node. A minimal configuration file is:

```
rules:
- pattern: ".*"
```

Check the Prometheus documentation (*https://oreil.ly/n6a_K*) for more details on writing rules. Next, add the following line to your Presto coordinator *jvm.config* file to attach Prometheus to Presto:

```
javaagent:<path/to/jmx_prometheus_javaagent.jar=8081:<path/to/prometheus.yaml>
```

Prometheus will listen to the 8081 port. Change it if you prefer to use another port. Finally, start your Presto coordinator, enter it, and run the following command:

```
curl 0.0.0.0:8081
```

You should see a long output that starts with something similar to this:

```
# HELP com_facebook_presto_execution_RemoteTaskFactory_Executor_TaskCount
[...]
# TYPE com_facebook_presto_execution_RemoteTaskFactory_Executor_TaskCount
untyped com_facebook_presto_execution_RemoteTaskFactory_Executor_TaskCount 0.0
```

You can find a complete, working example in the book's GitHub repository under *06/jmx-exporter*. First, you must build a new Docker image in the *presto-docker* directory, and then you can run the Presto cluster, included in the *kubernetes* directory.

Management

Managing a Presto cluster involves a range of tasks and responsibilities that ensure the system is operating efficiently and effectively. Management includes resource groups, verifiers, session properties managers, and function namespaces.

Resource Groups

Presto uses resource groups to manage resource utilization in a multitenant environment. Resource groups allow you to enforce limits or quotas on what each group can do. The coordinator applies these limits when deciding whether to run a query. Using resource groups creates a penalty-based system that runs queries submitted by low-resource groups with a significant delay.

Presto configures resource groups hierarchically, where nonleaf groups can be further subdivided into multiple resource groups. However, only the lowest level subgroup of a given branch can designate resource limits.

Configuring resource groups

Enable resources groups by adding a file named *resource-groups.properties* to your Presto coordinator *etc* directory. This file points to an external JSON file that defines resource groups and their selector rules.

To enable resource groups in your local Presto cluster, add the following configuration properties to the *presto-config-map.yaml* file:

```
resource-groups.properties: |
    resource-groups.configuration-manager=file
    resource-groups.config-file=etc/resource_groups.json

resource_groups.json: |
    <put_here_the_resource_groups_and_the_selector_rules>
```

Then, add a volume mount point and a volume for both properties in the *presto-coordinator.yaml* file, as described in Chapter 2, and restart your Presto cluster.

Resource groups properties

In Presto, you can configure many resources. The most important ones involve CPU and memory usage. For a complete list of parameters, refer to the Presto documentation (*https://oreil.ly/e44QR*).

CPU

Presto measures CPU in terms of CPU time. When the time crosses a limit (softCpuLimit), Presto reduces the number of queries linearly until it reaches 0. This event happens when the time for the number of queries reaches the hardCpuLimit, which is always greater than softCpuLimit.

Presto uses the cpuQuotaPeriod property to define the period in which CPU quotas are enforced. For example, if a cluster had a cpuQuotaPeriod value set to one hour, then each quota group would be deducted the hardCpuLimit at the end of each period. However, the previous example assumes that there is a single worker node with a single core available. A cluster with 20 nodes, each having 16 cores, would have a total CPU time of 320 CPU hours per quota period.

Calculating the CPU time limits is tricky because Presto doesn't use the same units of measure for all the fields. For example, hardCpuLimit and softCpuLimit are measured in CPU time for the whole cluster. The cpuQuotaPeriod, instead, is measured in clock time. Therefore, as the cluster scales out horizontally or vertically, hard and soft CPU limits must be adjusted to reflect the new amount of CPU time available to the cluster.

Memory

The aggregated memory for queries within a group cannot exceed the softMemoryLimit for memory. When that occurs, Presto doesn't execute any new queries until the aggregated memory usage drops below the specified softMemory Limit. This policy blocks all further submitted queries within the same group.

Example

Consider the following scenario. There are two groups, online and offline.

Use the key rootGroups to define the list of groups in the JSON file:

```
{
  "rootGroups": [
    {
      "name": "offline"
    },
    {
      "name": "online"
    }

  ]
}
```

The offline group can use a maximum of 30% of memory, have a maximum of 1,000 queries in the queue, and run a maximum of 50 concurrent queries:

```
{
  "name": "offline",
  "softMemoryLimit": "30%",
  "maxQueued"          : 1000,
  "hardConcurrencyLimit": 50
}
```

The online group can use a maximum 70% of memory, have a maximum of 1,000 queries in the queue, and run a maximum of 200 concurrent queries:

```
{
  "name": "online",
  "softMemoryLimit": "70%",
  "maxQueued"          : 1000,
  "hardConcurrencyLimit": 200
}
```

Once you have defined the groups, determine the selectors for them:

```
{
  "rootGroups": [ ... ],
  "selectors": [
    {
      "name": "offline",
      "source": "spark-etl";
      "queryType": "SELECT"
    },
    {
      "name": "online",
      "user": "web application"
    }
  ]
}
```

The offline group involves the spark-etl source and refers only to SELECT. The online group involves the web application user.

Finally, set the CPU quota period to two hours:

```
{
  "rootGroups"      : [ ... ],
  "selectors": [ ...],
  "cpuQuotaPeriod": "2h"
  ]
}
```

Verifiers

Presto is an actively developed project. As a result, a new version is released approximately every other month, while a patch version comes out at most twice a week. Therefore, you must evaluate the latest version for changes and performance benefits if running your own Presto environment. Alternatively, use a managed service vendor to manage Presto versions automatically.

The Presto verifier manages Presto versions and ensures that the new version returns the same query results as the previous one. To validate that performance hasn't regressed beyond a certain threshold, use another tool called Benchto (*https://oreil.ly/ 2sixD*).

Figure 6-6 shows the architecture of a system using the Presto verifier.

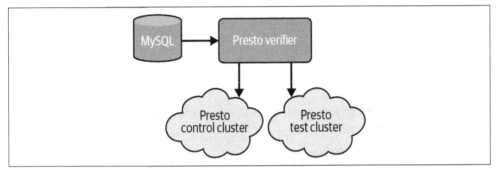

Figure 6-6. The architecture of a system using a Presto verifier

To configure a Presto verifier, you must maintain two clusters:

Control cluster
    The current running cluster

Test cluster
    The cluster with the new Presto version

The verifier compares the two clusters by running a set of queries you define manually into an external MySQL database.

Setting up the system

Create two instances of Presto in your local machine with MySQL and a TPC-H catalog. Refer to Chapter 2 for details. If your local machine does not have enough resources to run both clusters, deploy only the coordinator or deploy the two clusters in two separate machines.

1. Build a Presto Docker image using an old version of Presto, and name it `presto:<old_version>`.
2. Modify the *presto-coordinator.yaml* and *presto-workers.yaml* files to point to the `presto:<old_version>` image.
3. Deploy the Presto cluster under the namespace `presto-control`.

4. Repeat steps 1, 2, and 3 for the test cluster, paying attention to set the Presto version to the last version, the image name to `presto:<new_version>`, and the coordinator ports in the *presto-coordinator.yaml* file to 8081 and 8088. Deploy the Presto cluster under the namespace `presto-test`.

5. Download the Presto verifier JAR file and rename it *presto-verifier.jar*. Refer to the Presto documentation (*https://oreil.ly/XnFu8*) for the link to the last version.

Configuring the MySQL database

The Presto verifier uses a MySQL database:

1. Set up a MySQL instance as follows:

```
docker run --name testmysql -p 3306:3306\
-e MYSQL_ROOT_PASSWORD=root -d mysql:5.7
```

2. Enter your Docker image, run the `mysql` command, and create the database used by the Presto verifier:

```
CREATE DATABASE verify;
USE verify;
```

3. Create the table. The table contains information about the two clusters and the queries to verify.

```
CREATE TABLE verify.verifier_queries (
    id int(11) unsigned NOT NULL PRIMARY KEY AUTO_INCREMENT,
    suite varchar(256) NOT NULL,
    name varchar(256) DEFAULT NULL,
    control_catalog varchar(256) NOT NULL,
    control_schema varchar(256) NOT NULL,
    control_query text NOT NULL,
    control_username varchar(256) DEFAULT NULL,
    control_password varchar(256) DEFAULT NULL,
    control_session_properties text DEFAULT NULL,
    test_catalog varchar(256) NOT NULL,
    test_schema varchar(256) NOT NULL,
    test_query text NOT NULL,
    test_username varchar(256) DEFAULT NULL,
    test_password varchar(256) DEFAULT NULL,
    test_session_properties text DEFAULT NULL)
```

Configuring the Presto verifier

To run the Presto verifier properly, define the following configuration file, named *config.properties*:

1. Set the MySQL connector:

```
source-query.suites=suite
source-query.database=\
jdbc:mysql://localhost:3306/verify?user=root&password=root
```

2. Set the host and port to connect the control cluster:

```
control.hosts=localhost
control.http-port=8080
control.jdbc-port=8080
```

3. Set the host and port to connect the test cluster:

```
test.hosts=localhost
test.http-port=8081
test.jdbc-port=8081
```

4. Set the output log. For a more detailed log, set event-clients to json.

```
test-id=1
event-clients=human-readable
human-readable.log-file=event-log.log
```

Running a test

Consider the following test. The Presto verifier executes queries from a MySQL table, runs these against two separate Presto installations, and compares the results. It then denotes the query as success or failure based on the results from two clusters.

The Presto verifier runs only deterministic queries, so you can't run queries on the TPC-H catalog. Instead, copy the customer table of the TPC-H catalog to the MySQL catalog. Then, log in to the Presto coordinator and run the following SQL command in your Presto client:

```
CREATE DATABASE testdb;
CREATE TABLE mysql.testdb.customer
AS SELECT
    *
FROM tpch.tiny.customer
LIMIT 5;
```

Consider now the testmysql Docker container from Docker Desktop. This container is different from the MySQL catalog connected to the Presto cluster. The Presto verifier uses the testmysql container, independent of the Presto cluster.

1. Run the following query that inserts a test:

```
INSERT INTO verify.verifier_queries
  (suite, name,
   control_catalog, control_schema, control_query, control_username,
   test_catalog, test_schema, test_query, test_username)
  VALUE
  ("suite", "presto_test",
   "mysql", "testdb",
```

```
"select * from mysql.testdb.customer", "mysql-user",
"mysql", "testdb",
"select * from mysql.testdb.customer", "mysql-user");
```

2. Run the Presto verifier:

```
java -Xmx1G -jar presto-verifier.jar verify config.properties
```

3. Once the Presto verifier finishes, open the *event-log.log* file to see the results:

```
presto_test: SUCCEEDED
```

Refer to the Presto documentation (*https://oreil.ly/cTFKu*) for more details about the Presto verifier.

Session Properties Managers

Use session properties to control resource usage, enable or disable features, and change how queries run. To manage session properties, add the *session-property-config.properties* file to the *etc* directory of your Presto coordinator with the following content:

```
session-property-config.configuration-manager=file
session-property-manager.config-file=etc/session-property-config.json
```

Similarly to the resource group manager, the session property manager reads an external JSON file containing the configuration. This configuration file consists of a list of match rules, each specifying a list of conditions the query must satisfy and a list of session properties that should be applied by default. For the list of match rules and some examples on how to use them, refer to the Presto documentation (*https://oreil.ly/9sPvx*).

Configuring a session property manager

Add the following configuration properties to the *presto-config-map.yaml* file:

```
session-property-config.properties: |
    session-property-config.configuration-manager=file
    session-property-manager.config-file=etc/session-property-config.json

session-property-config.json: |
    <put_here_the_match_rules>
```

Then, add a volume mount point and a volume for both properties in the *presto-coordinator.yaml* file, as described in Chapter 2, and restart your Presto cluster.

Namespace Functions

Presto enables you to create custom functions to store and retrieve when needed. The possibility of reusing the code written for specific actions is high in large organizations with multiple departments. You may want only some individuals to create their functions, avoiding code proliferation across the organizations. You can use namespace managers to manage the set of reusable functions to be stored and retrieved.

A function namespace groups functions into logical segments. It also enables operators to define the same functions with slightly different behaviors or logic that will take effect based on which user submits the query. For example, the date-time conversion logic for a team residing in Asia may not need to consider daylight saving time, whereas a team in the US will. Presto abstracts function namespaces to look like schemas from other Presto catalogs, but they don't have the same behavior.

Presto ties any function (except built-in functions) to a function namespace and then registers it to that namespace along with specific defining characteristics about its metadata. To refer to a function, use its namespace, function name, and parameters, as described later in this section.

Function namespaces are also read-only, so you can't define a function or drop the namespace at runtime.

Function Namespaces Versus SPI Functions

Function namespaces differ from the Presto SPI functions you have seen in Chapter 3. Function namespaces are high-level functions that enable you to write custom functions. SPI functions are low-level functions that map the SQL syntax to the native catalog syntax. For example, let's suppose you have defined the following function using the function namespace: `tan(x) = sin(x)/cos(x)`. You can use this function only to query catalogs that support `sin(x)` and `cos(x)`.

Setting up the system

Presto stores function namespaces into a MySQL catalog. In our scenario, we use the MySQL catalog already configured in Chapter 2. Use the code contained in the *06/function-namespace* directory in the book's GitHub repository to configure the scenario.

1. Presto stores the configuration files used for function namespaces in a folder named *function-namespace*, contained in the *etc* directory within the server home. To enable function namespaces in our scenario, add the following configuration string to the *presto-secrets.yaml* file. Use the same username and password as your MySQL catalog.

   ```
   funcatalog.properties: |
       function-namespace-manager.name=mysql
       database-url=\
       jdbc:mysql://mysql:3306/functionsdb?user=root&password=dbuser
   ```

```
function-namespaces-table-name=example_function_namespaces
functions-table-name=example_sql_functions
```

2. Mount the *funcatalog.properties* file in the *presto-coordinator.yaml* and *presto-workers.yaml* files:

```
containers:
  - name: presto-coordinator
    volumeMounts:
      - name: funcatalog
        mountPath:
          "/opt/presto/etc/function-namespace/funcatalog.properties"
        subPath: funcatalog.properties
volumes:
  - name: funcatalog
    secret:
      secretName: presto-mysql-secrets
```

3. Ensure you have the *mysql.properties* file properly configured, connecting to this database as a standard database connector.

4. Restart your cluster.

Configuring a function

We'll configure a sample function, named `tan()`, that receives a `double` as an input and returns its tangent trigonometric function. We'll insert this function into a namespace called `math`.

Connect to the Presto coordinator and run the Presto client. Insert a new namespace, named `math`, into your catalog:

```
INSERT INTO
  mysql.functionsdb.example_function_namespaces
    (catalog_name, schema_name)
  VALUES ('funcatalog', 'math');
```

You have created a catalog named `funcatalog` and a schema named `math`. This process is just like you develop standard catalogs and schemas for tables.

Define the function `tan(x)`:

```
CREATE OR REPLACE FUNCTION
  funcatalog.math.tan(x double)
  RETURNS double DETERMINISTIC
  RETURNS NULL ON NULL INPUT
  RETURN sin(x)/cos(x);
```

Running a test

Run the following query:

```
SELECT funcatalog.math.tan(totalprice)
FROM tpch.tiny.orders
LIMIT 1;
```

The query produces the following output:

```
         _col0
--------------------
 -1.2274920493551589
(1 row)

Query 20221229_162154_00003_u6833, FINISHED, 1 node
Splits: 37 total, 37 done (100.00%)
0:35 [15K rows, 0B] [427 rows/s, 0B/s]
```

Conclusion

In this chapter, you learned how to administer Presto in three steps: configuration, monitoring, and management.

Configuration enables setting up the cluster before deploying it. Presto supports three types of configurations: properties, sessions, and JVM.

Monitoring helps you to identify potential issues or problems with the system and take appropriate action to resolve them. You can use three tools to monitor your Presto cluster: Presto console, REST API, and metrics.

Management enables you to maximize the performance of your Presto cluster. It includes tasks such as resource utilization, system updates, session managers, and function namespaces.

Understanding Security in Presto

Securing a Presto cluster involves building secure communication, authenticating the parties involved, and authorizing actors. Secure communication is the process of exchanging information between two parties to prevent unauthorized access to the data. Authentication verifies that users are who they claim to be, and authorization grants access to resources based on the user's identity.

The chapter is organized into four parts. In the first part, we'll define the scenario we'll implement throughout the chapter. Next, you'll learn how to build secure communication in Presto through encryption, keystore management, and HTTPS/TLS. In the third part, we'll focus on three types of authentication: file-based authentication, LDAP-based authentication, and Kerberos-based authentication. Finally, you'll learn how to manage authorization in Presto through system access control and Apache Ranger.

Introducing Presto Security

In previous chapters, we assumed that our cluster of nodes was trusted and that there were no threats from the outside. This trustworthiness is because we have considered that all the nodes belonging to the cluster work together, and there is no unauthorized access to the data. In a real environment, however, this is not true. A cluster can be subject to various attacks, including unauthorized access to data, data theft, data corruption, or even service disruption. In a worst-case scenario, the cluster could become completely unusable, resulting in costly downtime and significant data losses. These threats highlight the importance of implementing secure communication protocols to protect the cluster.

Consider the scenario described in Figure 7-1. There is a trusted simplified data lake-house, composed of two Presto clients, A and B; one Presto coordinator; one Presto worker; and two catalogs, TPC-H and MySQL. In the remainder of this chapter, we will implement this trusted data lakehouse to prevent the untrusted client and Presto worker from accessing it. In addition, we will implement an authorization policy that will enable Presto client A to access only the TPC-H catalog, and Presto client B to access only the MySQL catalog.

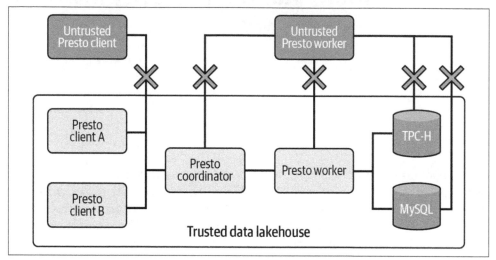

Figure 7-1. A trusted data lakehouse scenario

Building Secure Communication in Presto

Secure communication ensures that the data remains safe and confidential within the cluster. Secure communication involves using encryption protocols to encode the data, and authentication methods to verify users' identities before granting them access to the data.

Encryption

There are two types of encryption: symmetric and asymmetric. Symmetric encryption encodes data with a key, so only those who know that key can decipher the data. In asymmetric encryption, there are two keys, one for encryption (public key) and the other for decryption (private key). The sender encrypts data using the receiver's public key, and the receiver deciphers data using their private key. Presto uses asymmetric encryption. In any distributed environment, including a Presto cluster, you can implement two types of encryption: encryption over the wire and encryption at REST:

Encryption over the wire

All data over the wire is encrypted, so malicious attackers can't simply tap into the network and read the data transmitted over the wire. TLS (Transport Layer

Security)/HTTPS is the industry-standard way of ensuring encryption. Presto supports two types of encryption over the wire: between the client and the Presto coordinator and between the Presto coordinator and the Presto workers.

Encryption at REST

All data is encrypted on storage, so only those with the correct keys can access it. Therefore, Presto has little control over the REST destination or source system encryption. However, Presto must be able to read and write encrypted data from these sources, be they RDBMS, analytical systems, or object stores.

Describing encryption at REST is out of the scope of this book since it depends on the specific source. In the remainder of the section, we will focus on encryption over the wire. You can find the code described in this section in the *07/presto-https* directory in the book's GitHub repository.

Keystore Management

To implement encryption over the wire, you need digital certificates. A digital certificate verifies the identity of individuals, servers, or other entities in a network. There are various ways to obtain a digital certificate, such as using your hosting or cloud provider, obtaining a free certificate from Let's Encrypt (*https://oreil.ly/rckLV*), or generating a self-signed certificate.

In this chapter, we'll use `keytool` to generate a self-signed certificate. The main disadvantage of a self-signed certificate is that most clients and devices do not trust it by default, which can result in security warnings and errors when trying to establish secure connections. Thus, in a real scenario, you should obtain certificates from a certification authority.

Keytool enables you to manage digital certificates, keys, and passwords in Java. To generate a new certificate, run the following command for each node in the cluster, making sure to set the `alias` to the node name:

```
keytool -genkeypair -alias presto-coordinator \
-dname CN=presto-coordinator -keyalg RSA \
-keystore presto-coordinator-keystore.jks \
-ext "SAN=dns:presto-coordinator,dns:localhost"
```

To also access the Presto coordinator from the local Presto client, add `localhost` and `127.0.0.1` as a Subject Alternative Name (SAN) when creating the certificate. Fill out the form. At the end of the procedure, `keytool` generates a file named *presto-keystore.jks* containing your Java Keystore File.

So far, you have obtained a certificate for every node in the cluster. To securely communicate with the other cluster nodes, every cluster node must import the certificates of the other nodes in the same cluster. For example, if you have three nodes, A, B, and C, A must import B and C certificates into its keystore, B must import A and C certificates, and C must import A and B certificates. To import a certificate into the keystore of the other nodes, first extract the certificate from its original keystore, and then import it into the keystores of the other nodes:

```
keytool -exportcert -alias presto-coordinator \
-keystore presto-coordinator-keystore.jks -rfc -file presto-coordinator.pem
keytool -importcert -alias presto-coordinator \
-keystore presto-worker-keystore.jks -file presto-coordinator.pem
```

The next step involves copying the *presto-keystore.jks* file to all the cluster nodes. In our case, we can specify it in the Kubernetes configuration file of the coordinator and workers. For example, we can mount the *presto-keystore.jks* file as an additional volume in the *presto-coordinator.yaml* file:

```
spec:
  containers:
  - name: presto-coordinator
  ....
  volumeMounts:
  - name: certificate
  mountPath: "/opt/presto/etc/presto-keystore.jks"

  volumes:
  - name: certificate
  hostPath:
  path: "/path/to/presto-keystore.jks"
```

Configuring HTTPS/TLS

Let's start by securing the external communication between the Presto coordinator and the clients. To do this, enable HTTPS in the Presto coordinator as follows. First, modify the *config.properties* file in the Presto coordinator to enable HTTPS and disable HTTP. Also, set the HTTPS port (`http-server.https.port`), the path to the certificate (`http-server.https.keystore.path`), and the password to access the certificate (`http-server.https.keystore.key`):

```
http-server.http.enabled=false
http-server.https.enabled=true
http-server.https.port=8443
http-server.https.keystore.path=/path/to/certificate.p12
http-server.https.keystore.key=password
```

Next, configure the nodes to communicate using the fully qualified domain name (FQDN). The FQDN assigns a complete and unique address to every cluster node:

```
node.internal-address-source=FQDN
node.internal-address=<node address>
```

For example, for the coordinator, set the `node.internal-address` to `presto-coordinator`.

Now we can configure secure communication for the internal communication between the Presto coordinator and the workers:

```
internal-communication.https.required=true
internal-communication.https.keystore.path=/path/to/presto-keystore.jks
internal-communication.https.keystore.key=password
```

Finally, start the Presto coordinator.

Running a Presto client

Run the Presto client inside the coordinator, passing the Presto coordinator address and the port:

```
presto --server https://presto-coordinator:8443 --truststore-path \
/opt/presto/etc/presto-keystore.jks --truststore-password password
```

You also must pass the certificate to the Presto client because it's self-signed. If a certification authority had signed the certificate, the Presto client would not have required it because it would have recognized the certificate as being trusted by a trusted third party.

Performance Degradation

Encryption can impact performance depending on the environment, queries, and concurrency.

Running the Presto console

Open the browser and point it to *https://localhost:8443*. Don't be alarmed that your browser still reports the communication as insecure because it uses a self-signed certificate, not one from a trusted certificate authority. Proceed anyway and access your Presto console.

Authentication

Authentication is verifying a user's identity to ensure they are who they claim to be. Authentication in Presto requires encryption over the wire to be enabled.

Presto supports three types of authentication: file-based authentication, Lightweight Directory Access Protocol (LDAP)–based authentication, and Kerberos-based authentication. You can use the first two types of authentication to authenticate a Presto client to the Presto coordinator and the Kerberos-based authentication to authenticate a Presto client to the Presto coordinator and to authenticate the Presto coordinators and the Presto workers.

File-Based Authentication

File-based authentication allows you to grant access to a Presto cluster based on usernames and passwords stored in a file. To configure this type of authentication, you must have HTTPS enabled in your Presto cluster. You can find the code described in this section in the *07/presto-file-based-authentication* directory in the book's GitHub repository.

Let's start by generating the list of usernames and passwords. Use the `htpasswd` command provided by the `apache-utils` or `bcrypt` tool.

Installing htpasswd

You can install the `bcrypt` tool by running the following command: `yum -y install bcrypt` (Centos), `apt-get install bcrypt` (Ubuntu), or `brew install bcrypt` (macOS). Alternatively, you can install `bcrypt` through Node.js.

Generate the password for two accounts, one for each client of the scenario described in Figure 7-1, and save them into a file named *password.db*:

```
touch password.db
htpasswd -B -C 10 password.db clientA
htpasswd -B -C 10 password.db clientB
```

Use the `-C` option to set the computing time for the `bcrypt` algorithm. Presto requires a minimum value of 8. The *password.db* file contains the hashed password for each username. The following snippet of code shows an example of the output:

```
clientA:$2y$10$6/Z9xkk4XJYcUXP3xdHx9O3wZ/vtUz8uMZYlz0YwMJLAea0c3OLI2
clientB:$2y$10$WkrVISM7cX6rSttnWc5bFuH1mXMKUJ1GNOq9xUIpi1k3L.1dKW8.u
```

Once you have generated the passwords, configure Presto to enable file-based authentication. Add the following line the *config.properties* file:

```
http-server.authentication.type=PASSWORD,CERTIFICATE
```

Next, add a file named *password-authenticator.properties* in the *etc* directory of your Presto installation:

```
password-authenticator.name=file
file.password-file=</path/to/password.db>
```

You can specify `password-authenticator.properties` as an additional string of the Presto `configMap` in the Kubernetes configuration. Then, configure the *presto-coordinator.yaml* file to mount the `password-authenticator.properties` string as a volume and the *password.db* file as an external volume. Refer to the book's GitHub repository for more details.

Running a Presto client

When you run a Presto client, you must specify the credentials to access Presto. For example, when using the Presto CLI, add the --user and --password parameters:

```
presto \
  --server https://presto-coordinator:8443 \
  --truststore-path /opt/presto/etc/presto-keystore.jks \
  --truststore-password password \
  --user clientA \
  --password
```

You should be able to run any query. Instead, if you try to log in using a client not registered in the *password.db* file, such as clientC, you can still enter the Presto shell. However, you get a message about invalid credentials if you try to run any query:

```
presto \
  --server https://presto-coordinator:8443 \
  --truststore-path /opt/presto/etc/presto-keystore.jks \
  --truststore-password password \
  --user clientC \
  --password
Password:
presto> show catalogs;
Error running command: Authentication failed: Access Denied: Invalid credentials
```

Running the Presto console

Open the browser and point it to the Presto coordinator (*https://localhost:8443*). Presto now prompts for authentication via a username/password dialog. Use the username *clientA* or *clientB* and the password you set earlier to authenticate with Presto (Figure 7-2).

Figure 7-2. The authentication dialog box in the Presto console

LDAP

LDAP is an industry-standard protocol for directory-service authentication. You can use the LDAP service to authenticate users who want to access Presto. Add an LDAP service to your trusted lakehouse to make your Presto coordinator use LDAP authentication, as shown in Figure 7-3. The client logs in to the Presto coordinator through a username and a password. The Presto coordinator then validates the credentials with the external LDAP service and creates the principal associated with the provided username. Installing an LDAP service is out of the scope of this book. However, you can use FreeIPA (*https://oreil.ly/Myqkq*) to run some tests.

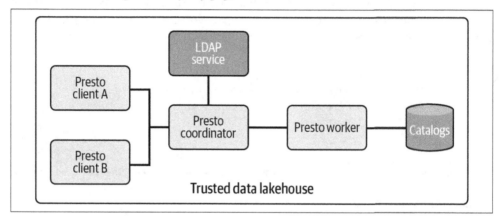

Figure 7-3. Adding an LDAP service to the trusted lakehouse

Once your LDAP service is running, configure the Presto coordinator for authentication with LDAP. Edit the *password-authenticator.properties* file as follows:

```
password-authenticator.name=ldap
ldap.url=ldaps://<url_to_the_ldap_service>:636
ldap.user-ldap.user-bind-pattern=<your_bind_pattern>
```

For example, if you use LDAP with Active Directory, set the `ldap.user-ldap.user-bind-pattern` as follows:

```
ldap.user-ldap.user-bind-pattern=${USER}@<your domain name>
```

At runtime, the `${USER}` will be replaced by the actual user performing authentication. Alternatively, you can define a user ID:

```
ldap.user-ldap.user-bind-pattern=
+uid=${USER},cn=users,cn=accounts,dc=ipa,dc=test
```

Restart the Presto coordinator and connect using the LDAP credentials.

Kerberos

Kerberos ensures mutual authentication between a client and a server using a *ticket* system that verifies user identity. Presto supports both external and internal authentication. External authentication is between a Presto client and the Presto coordinator. Internal authentication is between the Presto coordinator and the Presto workers. Installing a Kerberos server is out of the scope of this book. In this section, we assume that you have a running Kerberos server instance.

Kerberos Versus LDAP

Although both provide user and service authentication, Kerberos and LDAP were invented for different purposes. Kerberos is used for its single sign-on (SSO) capabilities and secure transmission of credentials over an insecure network. LDAP, instead, provides a directory service that stores and organizes information about users, devices, network objects, and other resources in a network.

Prerequisites

Figure 7-4 displays the Presto nodes of a Kerberos-enabled lakehouse. All the nodes involved in the authentication process must be configured to connect to the Kerberos server. Each Kerberos client node uses the *keytab* file and the *etc/krb5.conf* file. The *keytab* file contains pairs of encrypted keys and their corresponding usernames or service names. The */etc/krb5.conf* file contains settings related to domain authentication, encryption algorithms, and other parameters.

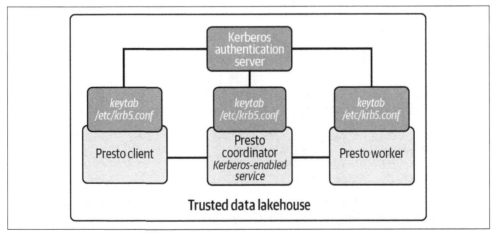

Figure 7-4. Adding a Kerberos server to the trusted lakehouse

The /etc/krb5.conf file must define the [realm] section, containing at least the kdc parameter:

```
[realms]
  PRESTO.MYDOMAIN.COM = {
    kdc = kdc.mydomain.com
  }

[domain_realm]
  .presto.mydomain.com = PRESTO.MYDOMAIN.COM
  presto.mydomain.com = PRESTO.MYDOMAIN.COM
```

You can also specify the Presto domain in the [domain_realm] section.

Configuring the Presto coordinator and workers

First, enable HTTPS by following the instructions in "Configuring HTTPS/TLS" on page 118. Then modify the *config.properties* file of the Presto coordinator and workers to enable Kerberos:

```
http-server.authentication.type=KERBEROS
http.server.authentication.krb5.service-name=presto
http.server.authentication.krb5.service-hostname=presto.mydomain.com
http.server.authentication.krb5.keytab=</path/to/keytab>
http.authentication.krb5.config=/etc/krb5.conf
```

If you want to use Kerberos only for external configuration, don't modify the *config.properties* file of the workers and leave HTTP enabled. You can find more information about configuring the Presto coordinator with Kerberos in the Presto documentation (*https://oreil.ly/f4Byj*).

Configuring the Presto client

Launch the Presto CLI with the krb5-* parameters:

```
presto \
  --server https://presto-coordinator:8443 \
  --truststore-path /opt/presto/etc/presto-keystore.jks \
  --truststore-password password \
  --krb5-config-path /etc/krb5.conf \
  --krb5-principal clientA@MYDOMAIN.COM \
  --krb5-keytab-path /path/to/keytab \
  --krb5-remote-service-name presto
```

You can find more information about configuring a Presto client with Kerberos in the Presto documentation (*https://oreil.ly/nxGCc*).

Creating a Custom Authenticator

You can implement a custom authentication service in Presto using the SPI provided by Presto. In Chapter 3, you learned how to implement a custom connector in

Presto. In the case of a custom authentication service, you can use the security classes (*https://oreil.ly/30bZN*) provided by the Presto SPI. For example, to define a custom password authenticator, implement the `PasswordAuthenticator` interface:

```
public class MyAuthenticator
        implements PasswordAuthenticator{
    ...
}
```

Take LDAP Authenticator (*https://oreil.ly/YiKhq*) as a reference for your custom password authenticator. Also, make sure that HTTPS is enabled when you implement your custom authentication service.

Authorization

Authorization gives a user permission to do or have something. An authenticated user can only access sources and destinations to which they have access.

Authorizing Access to the Presto REST API

Authorization at a system level defines the access control policies at a global level before any connector-level authorization. You can either use one of the built-in plug-ins in Presto or implement your own by following the guidelines in the Presto documentation (*https://oreil.ly/mfcO_*). Presto offers three built-in plug-ins: allow-all (default), read-only, and file (customizable) access.

In Chapter 4, we saw different ways to connect a Presto client to Presto, including the Presto REST API. For example, you can enable authorization via HTTP REST endpoints to control who has access to which HTTP endpoint in Presto.

Presto defines three main roles:

User
> Users who need access to the external Presto endpoints to launch queries, check status, and receive or provide data for the UI

Internal
> The Presto worker and coordinator, which need access to endpoints to launch tasks on workers or move data from one worker to another

Admin
> System administrators who need access to internal service endpoints, for example, to get node status

To configure authorization, first enable authentication. You have already learned how to enable authentication in the previous sections. In this section, we use file-based authentication. Next, configure an authorizer. You can use the default authorizer provided by Presto, `ConfigurationBasedAuthorizer`, or implement your custom authorizer as a Presto plug-in. Refer to the Presto documentation (*https://oreil.ly/ 77C76*) to configure your custom authorizer.

Configuring System Access Control

Presto defines a system access control plug-in to enforce authorization at a global level. You can define your custom plug-in or use the default plug-ins provided by Presto. Presto offers three built-in plug-ins: *allow-all*, *read_only*, and *file*. The last plug-in lets you define your custom rules in a configuration file. For more details on system access control, refer to the Presto documentation (*https://oreil.ly/dWGrN*).

Consider the scenario described in Figure 7-1. The objective is to create rules so that `clientA` can read the `tpch` catalog and `clientB` can read the `mysql` catalog. Refer to the *07/presto-authorization* directory in the book's GitHub repository for more details on the code. To enable access control, add a file named *access-control.properties* in the *etc* directory of the Presto coordinator. When you enable file-based access control, Presto will deny access to catalogs unless a specific rule for a user explicitly permits them. In the *access-control.properties* file, specify the type of access control you want to use (`file`, in our case) and the path to the file containing the rules:

```
access-control.name=file
security.config-file=/path/to/rules.json
```

You must specify rules in JSON. Refer to the Presto documentation (*https://oreil.ly/ L8x3Q*) for more details. In our scenario, we want to enable `clientA` to read the `tpch` catalog and `clientB` to read the `mysql` catalog. So, let's add the following rules to the JSON file:

```
{
    "catalogs": [
        {
            "user": "clientA",
            "catalog": "tpch",
            "allow": "read-only"
        },
        {
            "user": "clientB",
            "catalog": "mysql",
            "allow": "read-only"
        }
    ]
}
```

Under the `catalogs` section, add the list of rules referring to access to catalogs. Next, restart the Presto cluster and log in to the Presto CLI as client A, as described in the previous section. You should be able to see the TPC-H catalog but not the MySQL catalog. Likewise, if you log in to the Presto CLI as client B, you should be able to see the MySQL catalog but not the TPC-H catalog.

```
presto \
  --server https://presto-coordinator:8443 \
  --truststore-path /opt/presto/etc/presto-keystore.jks \
  --truststore-password password \
  --user clientA \
  --password
Password:
presto> show catalogs;
 Catalog
---------
 system
 tpch
(2 rows)
```

Authorization Versus Access Control

Access control in Presto regulates the access to Presto resources, such as catalogs, schemas, tables, columns, and data. You can configure access control policies in Presto at various levels, such as the server, catalog, schema, or table level. On the other hand, authorization in Presto is the default set of permissions and access control rules that Presto automatically enforces for the available resources.

Consider a table with three columns: user, password, and number of bought items. A possible authorization policy ensures that only authorized employees of a company can connect to the Presto cluster and see the table. Access control specifies a more fine-grained policy. For example, the data team can write and read all three table columns, and analysts can read only the column number of bought items.

Authorization Through Apache Ranger

Granting users access control is configurable at a connector level. You can do this through the source system or authorization services like Apache Ranger via the Hive plug-in. This section will use Apache Ranger to implement connector-level security.

Apache Ranger (*https://oreil.ly/ahrV_*) is an open source authorization service supporting fine-grained access control and audit capabilities for data platforms through centralized security administration. Apache Ranger's open data governance model and plug-in architecture enable access control extension to projects beyond the Hadoop ecosystem. The platform is widely used among significant cloud vendors, including AWS, Azure, and GCP.

Figure 7-5 shows the architecture of a system that integrates Presto and Ranger. Ranger uses a database to store policies and provides a module to manage an audit. To make Presto use Ranger, you must install a Ranger plug-in in Presto. In addition, you can configure Presto to send logs to the audit database.

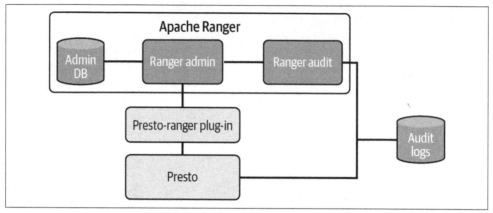

Figure 7-5. How to integrate Presto and Ranger

Ranger provides the Presto Hive plug-in to connect to Presto. Use this plug-in only for Hive connector-based catalogs like Hive Metastore and AWS Glue. Set up a network communication between your Presto cluster and Ranger instance to use the Hive connector with Ranger. The Hive connector supports Apache Ranger 2.1.0 or later. For more details on how to set up the Ranger plug-in for Hive, read the Presto documentation (*https://oreil.ly/s4QT1*) to configure the Ranger plug-in for Presto.

Building a custom audit function

An audit function monitors and tracks activities within your data lakehouse to ensure compliance with regulations, policies, and standards. Before building an audit function, you must define the requirements by identifying the events you want to audit, such as data access, data modifications, or user logins, and the level of detail you need to capture. Next, identify the audit data sources you will use to capture the audit data, such as Presto logs or Ranger audit logs. Finally, implement the audit function using a service like Ranger. Refer to the Ranger documentation (*https://oreil.ly/h4ZZM*) for more details to configure an audit function using Ranger.

Conclusion

In this chapter, you learned how to configure security in Presto by building secure communication, setting up authentication, and configuring authorization.

Secure communication in Presto is an encryption feature ensuring that any data sent through Presto remains secure. To build secure communication in Presto, you must configure HTTPS/TLS.

Authentication in Presto ensures that only authorized users can access the Presto service. In Presto, you can set up authentication through file-based authentication, LDAP, or Kerberos. You can also write a custom authenticator.

Authorization grants users access to specific catalogs, schemas, or tables, and limits their ability to perform certain actions. In Presto, you can implement authorization through system access control or external services like Apache Ranger.

Performance Tuning

Performance tuning involves optimizing the performance of your Presto cluster by making small adjustments to improve its speed, efficiency, and overall performance. This process starts by analyzing the existing system to determine where and how to improve. Once we have identified the areas for improvement, we can implement changes to maximize performance.

The chapter is organized into five parts. In the first part, we'll introduce some basic concepts related to performance tuning, including motivation and the performance tuning life cycle. In the second part, we'll see the Presto query execution model, which helps you understand where to act when there are bottlenecks. Next, we'll analyze some popular approaches for performance tuning in Presto, including resource allocation, storage, and query optimization. In the fourth part, we'll focus on Aria Scan, a project to improve Presto's performance by increasing table scan efficiency. Finally, we'll implement a practical use case to show how to tune some configuration parameters in Presto.

Introducing Performance Tuning

As you have learned in the previous chapters, Presto is a distributed query engine that enables you to query large datasets stored in multiple data sources. As the size and complexity of datasets grow, it becomes increasingly important to optimize the query execution process to minimize query response time and ensure the timely availability of data to users. Performance tuning identifies and addresses performance bottlenecks that may slow down the system, reduce its efficiency, or make it unstable.

Reasons for Performance Tuning

The performance tuning life cycle is a loop that continuously monitors the system performance and adjusts the configuration parameters whenever needed. There are many reasons to do performance tuning in Presto, including:

Access more data
> Presto handles an increased workload and delivers the required performance level to access, analyze, and process large and complex datasets from multiple data sources.

Improve response time
> Presto executes queries faster and more efficiently. This is especially beneficial in real-time environments where timely data access is required.

Save resources
> Presto reduces resource consumption by better utilizing the available resources, including hardware and network infrastructure.

The Performance Tuning Life Cycle

Presto's performance tuning life cycle involves four steps, as Figure 8-1 shows.

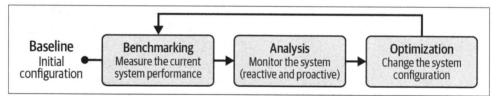

Figure 8-1. The performance tuning life cycle in Presto

Baseline
> Start by configuring Presto with an initial configuration with default values.

Benchmarking
> The first phase involves measuring the current system performance in terms of query response times, the number of nodes in the cluster, and the number of resources used during query execution.

Analysis
> The second phase involves monitoring the system to identify performance bottle-necks. Monitoring includes examining query plans, looking for slow queries, and identifying resource-intensive queries. There are two types of monitoring: *proactive* and *reactive*. Proactive monitoring involves periodically checking the system's performance by measuring CPU and memory utilization. Reactive monitoring identifies system bottlenecks and tries to fix them.

Optimization
    The third phase involves changing the system configuration to optimize the performance based on the analysis results.

Query Execution Model

Before describing how to improve the performance of a Presto cluster, we'll focus on how Presto executes a query. Understanding the Presto query execution model enables you to identify the possible causes of performance issues and optimize the query plan accordingly. With a clear understanding of the execution model, performance-tuning efforts are more likely to yield the desired results.

Figure 8-2 shows the query execution model in Presto.

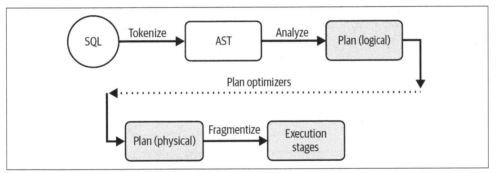

Figure 8-2. The query execution model in Presto

When the Presto coordinator receives an SQL statement from a Presto client, it parses and analyzes it. Then, it generates an internal data structure/format called Abstract Syntax Tree (AST), which is translated into a query execution plan. The query execution plan is composed of two parts: the logical and the physical plans. The logical plan is a high-level representation of the query independent of the underlying data sources and the specifics of the execution environment. It focuses on the logical structure of the query, such as the operations to be performed and the relationships between them. The physical plan is a detailed representation of the query that considers the specifics of the execution environment, such as the number of nodes, the network topology, and the available resources.

The query execution plan is composed of stages, splits, and tasks:

Stage
    A portion of the query plan that can be executed in parallel. It is composed of one or more tasks. Usually, the coordinator creates and manages stages.

Split

A chunk of data a worker can process independently from other splits. Splits are the smallest unit of work in Presto.

Task

A unit of work that a single worker can execute. A task is composed of one or more splits. Usually, the coordinator creates and manages tasks.

The coordinator distributes this plan to Presto workers, which execute it and return the results to the coordinator. Any intermediate data and state are stored in memory to achieve better performance whenever possible. As each task completes, the coordinator updates the query status. When the query result is ready, the coordinator returns it to the client.

Consider the `tpch.tiny` schema and run the following query, which calculates the total price for each customer, orders the customers by decreasing total price, and shows only the first 10 customers:

```
SELECT c.custkey, c.name, sum(o.totalprice)
FROM customer c
JOIN orders o ON c.custkey = o.custkey
GROUP BY c.custkey, c.name
ORDER BY sum(o.totalprice)
DESC LIMIT 10;
```

Then, access the Presto console, as described in Chapter 6, select your query, and access the live plan. A possible output is composed of the following four stages:

Stage 3

Composed of just one task that scans the `customer` table.

Stage 2

Composed of five tasks (Figure 8-3), which scan the `orders` table (`ScanProject`), merge it with the `customer` table (`LocalExchange`) through the `InnerJoin` task, and finally compute projection (`Project`) and partial aggregation (`Aggregate`).

Stage 1

Composed of four tasks, which perform the final aggregation and compute the partial top 10 customers.

Stage 0

Composed of three tasks, calculating the final top 10 customers and returning the results.

Note that the number of splits and tasks for each stage may vary based on the cluster configuration, data distribution, and parallelism settings.

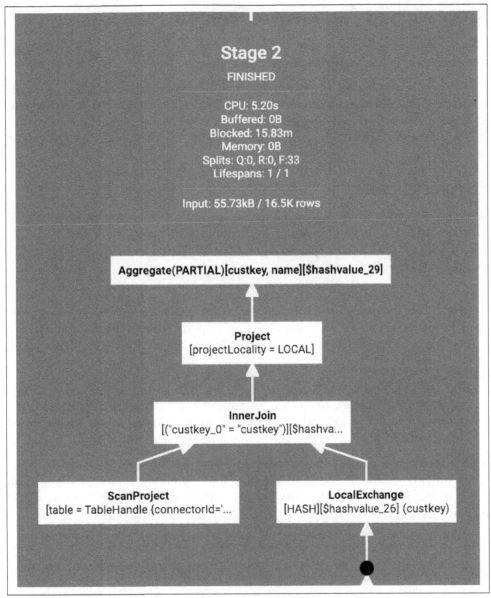

Figure 8-3. The structure of a possible Stage 2 in the Presto console

Approaches for Performance Tuning in Presto

There are three common approaches to improving query performance: allocate more resources, optimize data storage, and tune the query.

The first two approaches could improve resource bottlenecks, but that will only sometimes improve query performance. The third approach can be unpredictable, as the queries may be system generated, or it may take a lot of time to rewrite many application queries. The best solution is to take a holistic approach by adding resources and tuning Presto for maximum performance.

Resource Allocation

Resource allocation involves looking at the concurrency level and resource utilization. In most cases, increasing resource allocation is the quickest but not necessarily the cheapest way to get the query running faster. There are generally two ways to increase resource allocation:

Scale up or vertical scaling
> Involves increasing the resources of a single machine, such as adding more memory, CPU cores, or storage. Use this option when a single machine can handle the workload of the system but requires more resources than the current machine has.

Scale out or horizontal scaling
> Adds more instances or nodes to distribute the workload across multiple machines. Use this approach when a single server cannot handle the increased workload and adding more resources to a single node is not practical.

Regardless of your strategy to increase your resource allocation, you should understand which resources to increase. The choice of resources to allocate depends on the type of queries being performed. Table 8-1 outlines which resources you should increase based on the query type.

Table 8-1. Resources to increase depending on the query type

Query type	Queries examples	Resources to increase
Queries requiring large amounts of data to be stored in memory	Sorting large result sets, grouping or aggregating large datasets, joins involving large tables or multiple tables	Memory (e.g., use AWS R family, which is memory optimized)
Queries requiring a lot of processing power to execute	Complex calculations or functions, queries requiring a lot of data manipulation, recursive operations, multiple subqueries or nested queries, joins between large tables	CPU (e.g., use AWS C family, which is compute optimized)

There are two types of resources we can increase: memory and CPU.

Memory

To allocate more memory to a Presto node (coordinator and worker), modify the `-Xmx16G` property in the *jvm.config* file. For example, to allocate 60 GB to a Presto node, change `-Xmx16G` to `-Xmx60G`.

In addition, configure `query.max-memory-per-node` in the *config.properties* file. The default value of `query.max-memory-per-node` is 10% of the Xmx value specified in *jvm.config*. A good choice is setting `query.max-memory-per-node` to half of the JVM config max memory. However, if your workload is highly concurrent, use a lower value for `query.max-memory-per-node`.

For more details on the properties provided by Presto for memory management, refer to the Presto documentation (*https://oreil.ly/5JmV4*).

CPU

If your queries are CPU intensive, reducing concurrency can help reduce CPU pressure. In Presto, use the `task.concurrency` property in the *config.properties* file to set the number of vCPUs per node. The default value is 16. In the case of CPU-intensive queries, you may reduce the default value. For more details on the other task properties provided by Presto, refer to the Presto documentation (*https://oreil.ly/mJSM5*).

Reducing concurrency increases CPU availability, but it can also increase the wait time for query execution, as each query must wait its turn. Thus, you should balance query concurrency and CPU resource utilization.

Storage

Presto does not control the underlying data formats for data storage, nor does it have an indexing engine to index the location of data. So if the performance problem lies with storage, Presto can do little about it.

To solve the problem, you must act at the storage level. You can use compressed data formats containing information about the data in the file header (e.g., ORC and Parquet). While querying the underlying storage, Presto looks at the file headers to see if they match the query. If they don't, Presto skips them, thus resulting in faster query processing.

To improve performance, you can also enable *partitioning* at the storage level. Partitioning involves dividing a large dataset into smaller, more manageable subsets called partitions. Each partition is stored separately on the same or different nodes. In Presto, you can create a partitioned version of a table using Create Table As (CTAS) by adding the `partitioned_by` clause to the `CREATE TABLE`. For more details on CTAS, refer to the Presto documentation (*https://oreil.ly/fTEWU*).

Query Optimization

The Presto coordinator runs a query optimizer whenever it receives a new query from a client. The query optimizer simplifies the query plan by employing rule-based optimization and cost-based optimization strategies. In practice, the query optimizer iterates over a set of transformation rules to find the most optimal execution plan. Presto supports two query optimization strategies: predicate pushdown and cost-based optimization:

Predicate pushdown

> This strategy involves pushing down (i.e., moving) query predicates (i.e., conditions used to filter data) as close as possible to the data source, thereby reducing reads of unnecessary data, resulting in fewer I/O operations, reducing network traffic, and enabling faster execution time. Generally, this strategy helps join tables with `WHERE` clauses, where it's better to filter unnecessary data before joining them.
>
> Presto natively supports predicate pushdown. However, you can use this strategy only if the connector implements it. Read the article "Improving the Presto planner for better pushdown and data federation" (*https://oreil.ly/JnZ7p*) for more details on implementing a connector that supports predicate pushdown. For example, to enable predicate pushdown in S3 via a Hive connector, add the following configuration property to your catalog configuration file (i.e., *hive.properties*):
>
> ```
> hive.s3select-pushdown.enabled=true
> ```
>
> Read the Presto documentation (*https://oreil.ly/X1vvK*) for more details.

Cost-based optimizer (CBO)

> CBO aims to provide the most optimal query plan based on estimated costs and table statistics by considering the shape of the data to query. Based on the table statistics, CBO estimates the number of rows in the table and the average data size of the column. Then, it uses this information to determine the optimal join ordering strategy.
>
> Presto natively supports CBO. However, you can use this strategy only if the connector implements table statistics. Read the Presto documentation (*https://oreil.ly/GXNUC*) for more details about table statistics.
>
> Presto supports the following CBO strategies: join enumeration and join distribution selection. Join enumeration explores all possible join combinations to find the optimal order of joining tables in a query. Join distribution selection defines how to compute hash tables to perform joins. To enable a specific CBO strategy, you must set the associated property in the *config.properties* file or the corresponding session property. Table 8-2 outlines the supported CBO strategies,

the parameters to set in the *config.properties* file, the corresponding session properties, and the allowed values.

Read the Presto documentation (*https://oreil.ly/6GXwY*) for more details about CBO.

Table 8-2. CBO strategies and the associated parameters in Presto

CBO strategy	config.properties	Session property	Allowed values
Join enumeration	`optimizer.join-reordering-strategy`	`join_reordering_strategy`	AUTOMATIC (default), ELIMINATE_CROSS_JOINS, NONE
Join distribution selection	`optimizer.join-distribution-type`	`join_distribution_type`	AUTOMATIC (default), BROADCAST, PARTITIONED

Aria Scan

In 2019, Facebook launched Project Aria (*https://oreil.ly/sYDxi*), which achieved a two to three times reduction in CPU time needed for executing Hive queries on ORC-formatted tables. Project Aria concentrates on refining two areas: table scanning and repartitioning.

Table Scanning

A default table scan retrieves all the rows from a table when no indexes are available to satisfy a query. During a table scan, the query engine reads every row in the table, regardless of whether it meets the criteria specified in the query. Table scans can be slow and resource intensive, especially on large tables, as they involve reading and processing a large amount of data.

Aria reduces the CPU time required for table scans by using the following strategies: subfield pruning and filter pushdown:

Subfield pruning
Subfield pruning determines the table columns required by a query. If the query requires only a subset of the columns in a table, subfield pruning scans only those columns instead of reading the entire table.

In Presto, you can enable subfield pruning by setting the `experimental.pushdown-subfields-enabled` property to `true` in the *config.properties* file. Alternatively, set the `pushdown_subfields_enabled` session property to `true`.

Filter pushdown
Filter pushdown moves filter evaluation from the Presto engine to the Hive connector. This saves CPU time decoding unwanted rows and memory allocation for the materialized data.

In Presto, you can enable filter pushdown by setting the `<hive_catalog>`.`pushdown-filter-enabled` property to `true` in the *config.properties* file. For example, if the hive catalog's name is `hive`, set the `hive.pushdown-filter-enabled` property. Alternatively, set the `<hive_catalog>`.`pushdown_filter_enabled` session property to `true`.

Adaptive filter ordering improves the performance of queries involving multiple joins. It dynamically adjusts the join order based on some criteria, thus reducing the overall query time.

Repartitioning

Repartitioning in Presto refers to redistributing data across a set of workers in a Presto cluster. If Aria is not enabled, Presto performs repartitioning in two phases: build and serialization. During the build phase, Presto calculates a hash function on the partitioned column, and during the serialization step, it enqueues pages to the output buffer. However, if Aria is enabled, the build phase is eliminated, and Presto appends the data to buffers. Enabling Aria can reduce CPU consumption by about 50%.

In Presto, you can enable repartitioning by setting the `experimental.optimized-repartitioning` property in the *config.properties* file. Alternatively, set the `optimized_repartitioning` session property.

Use the configuration property `driver.max-page-partitioning-buffer-size` to control the size of the buffers, whose default value is 32 MB. The total buffer size for all partitions is limited by this number, and each buffer is also limited to 1 MB.

Implementing Performance Tuning

In this section, we'll show a strategy to implement performance tuning in a real scenario. We'll start from the scenario described in Figure 5-5 with the default configuration parameters, and then we'll test some of the parameters described in this chapter to improve the query elapsed time. Since the Aria scan only supports ORC files, we'll build a sample ORC table, and we'll import it into the MinIO object store. We'll use the Presto console, described in Chapter 6, to measure the test results.

We'll implement performance tuning in the following steps:

1. Building and importing the sample CSV table in MinIO
2. Converting the CSV table in ORC
3. Defining the tuning parameters
4. Running tests

Building and Importing the Sample CSV Table in MinIO

To run our tests, we'll extract a sample table from the TPC-H benchmark, and we'll import it into the MinIO object store. To do this, we'll connect a TPC-H catalog to Presto, read the `customer` table from the `sf1` schema in Presto, and export it to a CSV file. You can change the schema size to test a smaller or larger benchmark. Then, we'll import the CSV file into the MinIO object store, and we'll use Spark to convert the CSV format into ORC. We'll store the ORC table in the MinIO object store.

If you want to run tests directly, skip this section and use the sample CSV file available in the *08/data/customer.csv* directory in the book's GitHub repository.

1. Start your data lakehouse by running the command **./deploy.sh -d** and log in to the Presto coordinator. Add a *tpch.properties* file to the */opt/presto-server/etc/catalog* directory with the following content: `connector.name=tpch`.

2. Restart your Presto instance with the following commands:

   ```
   cd /opt/presto-server/bin
   ./launcher restart
   ```

   You'll be disconnected from the terminal. Enter it again from your Docker app.

3. To export the `customer` table into a CSV file, run the following command from the Presto coordinator:

   ```
   presto-cli \
   --execute "SELECT * FROM tpch.sf1.customer;" \
   --output-format CSV_HEADER > customer.csv
   ```

   Change `sf1` to your preferred size for a different benchmark. For `sf1`, you'll export a table with 150,000 rows.

4. To copy the *customer.csv* file to your host machine, install the `tar` package in your Presto coordinator with the following command: **yum install tar**. Then exit the Presto coordinator, and from your host machine, run the following command:

   ```
   kubectl cp\
    presto-coordinator-nm87g:/opt/presto-server/customer.csv\
    ./customer.csv
   ```

   Replace `presto-coordinator-nm87g` with the exact name of your Presto coordinator pod. You can obtain the pod name by running the command **kubectl get pods -n presto**.

5. Access the MinIO service at *http://localhost:9090/*. Insert your credentials and create a new path called `tpch` under the `warehouse` bucket. Upload the *customer.csv* file under *warehouse/tpch*.

Converting the CSV Table in ORC

Use Spark to convert the CSV `customer` table in ORC:

1. Log in to the Spark client and launch the Spark shell, as described in Chapter 5.

2. Import the required libraries:

```
import org.apache.hudi.QuickstartUtils._
import scala.collection.JavaConversions._
import org.apache.spark.sql.SaveMode._
```

3. Load the CSV `customer` table:

```
val tableName = "customer"
val basePath = "s3a://warehouse/tables/customer"
val df = spark.read.options(Map("header" -> "true")).
csv("s3a://warehouse/tpch/customer.csv")
```

4. Convert the CSV table into ORC and save it as `orc_customer`:

```
df.write.format("orc").
    options(getQuickstartWriteConfigs).
    option(RECORDKEY_FIELD_OPT_KEY, "id").
    option(PRECOMBINE_FIELD_OPT_KEY, "dob").
    option(TABLE_NAME, tableName).
    mode(Overwrite).
    saveAsTable("orc_customer")
```

Now you are ready to define the tuning parameters.

Defining the Tuning Parameters

Earlier in this chapter, you saw some of the most popular parameters for Presto tuning. We can classify those parameters into two main categories: enable/disable parameters and value-based parameters. For the enable/disable parameters, the only choice you can make is to enable or disable them. In contrast, for the value-based parameters, you can choose from a range of possible values. Table 8-3 shows the configuration parameters organized according to the described classification.

The table also shows in bold the parameters we'll tune in this section. We'll focus only on some representative parameters, but you can also use the described strategy to tune the other parameters.

Table 8-3. Enable/disable parameters and value-based parameters

Enable/disable parameters	Value-based parameters
hive.s3select-pushdown.enabled	query.max-memory-per-node
experimental.pushdown-subfields-enabled	**task.concurrency**
hive.pushdown-filter-enabled	optimizer.join-reordering-strategy
experimental.optimized-repartitioning	optimizer.join-distribution-type

Running Tests

To perform our tests, we'll run the following sample query:

```
SELECT count(*) as total, nationkey
FROM orc_customer
WHERE nationkey NOT IN ('23', '6')
GROUP KEY nationkey;
```

We'll test the following scenarios, and for each of them, we'll set the related properties and then run the sample query:

- Default parameters
- Reducing CPU usage
- Query optimization
- Aria scan

We'll use sessions to set parameters, and once we have found the best parameters for our scenario, we'll set them in the *config.properties* file.

Default parameters

Launch the Presto client from the Presto coordinator and run the sample query. Then, access the Presto console in your browser. Under the Query Details tab, click Finished, and then select your query. You can see the details of your query, including an overview of the query, the live plan, stage performance, and splits. Figure 8-4 shows the main statistics related to the default scenario, including the execution time, which is 8.14 seconds. This is the initial value we want to reduce.

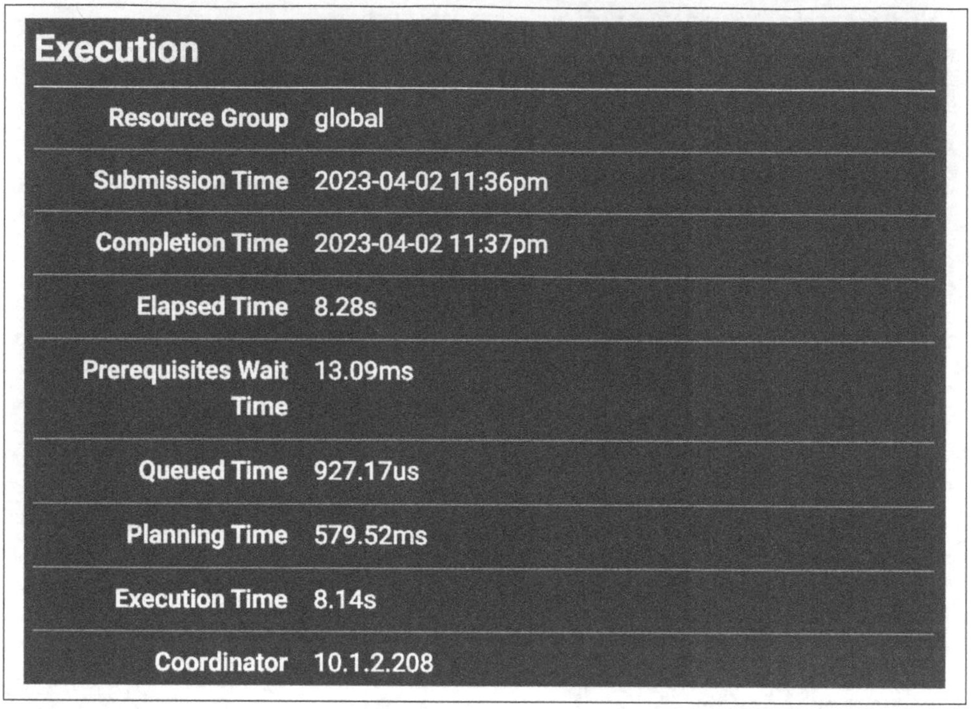

Execution	
Resource Group	global
Submission Time	2023-04-02 11:36pm
Completion Time	2023-04-02 11:37pm
Elapsed Time	8.28s
Prerequisites Wait Time	13.09ms
Queued Time	927.17us
Planning Time	579.52ms
Execution Time	8.14s
Coordinator	10.1.2.208

Figure 8-4. An overview of the default scenario

Reducing CPU usage

To lower the execution time, we can reduce CPU usage by decreasing the number of vCPUs. Reduce the `task.concurrency` parameter to 8 (the default value is 16):

```
SET SESSION task_concurrency = 8;
```

Then, run the sample query again. Figure 8-5 shows the main statistics related to the reducing CPU usage scenario, including the execution time, which is 6.67 sec. We have reduced the execution time by 1.47 sec.

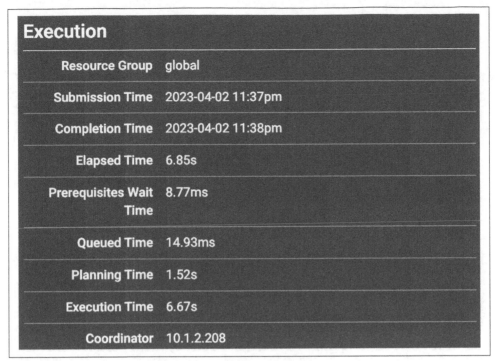

Figure 8-5. An overview of the reducing CPU usage scenario

Query optimization

To optimize the query, we can enable predicate pushdown and maintain the `task_concurrency` at 8:

```
SET SESSION hudi.s3_select_pushdown_enabled=true
```

Then, run the sample query again. Figure 8-6 shows the main statistics related to the query optimization scenario, including the execution time, which is 6.89 sec. This time is slower than that achieved without this property enabled. Thus, for this particular sample query, predicate pushdown does not help in reducing the execution time.

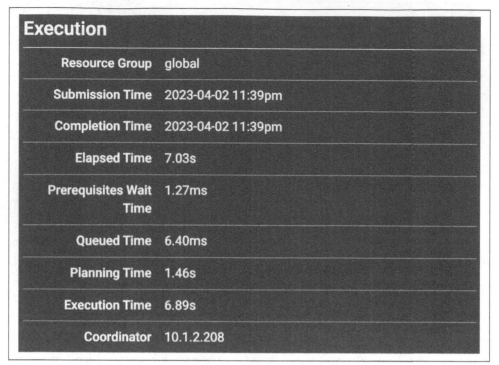

Figure 8-6. An overview of the query optimizing scenario

Aria scan

To optimize the query, we can enable filter pushdown and maintain the `task_con currency` at 8:

```
SET SESSION hudi.pushdown_filter_enabled = true;
```

Then, run the sample query again. Figure 8-7 shows the main statistics related to the query optimization scenario, including the execution time, which is 6.20 sec. We have reduced the execution time by 0.47 sec.

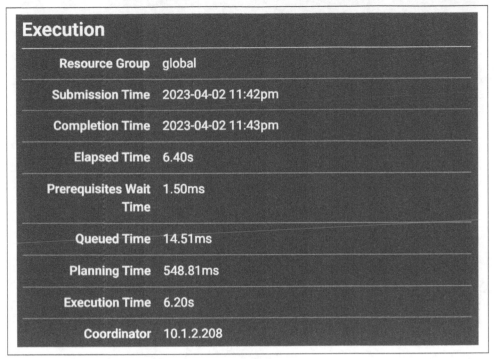

Execution	
Resource Group	global
Submission Time	2023-04-02 11:42pm
Completion Time	2023-04-02 11:43pm
Elapsed Time	6.40s
Prerequisites Wait Time	1.50ms
Queued Time	14.51ms
Planning Time	548.81ms
Execution Time	6.20s
Coordinator	10.1.2.208

Figure 8-7. An overview of the Aria scan scenario

At the end of our tests, we found the following configuration parameters in the *config.properties* file for reducing the execution time of the sample query:

```
task.concurrency = 8;
hudi.pushdown-filter-enabled = true;
```

Conclusion

In this chapter, you learned how to execute performance tuning in Presto. Performance tuning is a key factor in ensuring maximum efficiency and speed from your Presto cluster.

We discussed the basics of performance tuning and looked at the Presto query execution model. We also explored some popular approaches for optimizing performance, including resource allocation, storage, query optimization, and the Aria scan.

In the last part of the chapter, we implemented a case study on how to tune some configuration parameters in Presto.

Operating Presto at Scale

Scalability involves a Presto cluster handling increased demand or usage with minimal impact on performance, ensuring that the system's response time remains consistent and acceptable even when the workload increases.

We won't be implementing a specific scenario in this chapter, so you won't find the code in the book's GitHub repository since the scalability of your Presto cluster depends on your cluster workload. Instead, we'll discuss general strategies for scaling your Presto cluster to enable you to adapt them to your specific conditions.

The chapter is organized into four parts. In the first part, we'll introduce some basic concepts related to scalability, including reasons to scale a Presto cluster and some common issues related to a Presto cluster that needs to be scaled. In the second part, we'll see some design considerations to consider when you want to scale your Presto cluster. These include availability, manageability, performance, protection, and configuration. Next, we'll analyze popular approaches for scaling a Presto cluster, including multiple coordinators, Presto on Spark, and spilling. Finally, we'll focus on how to scale a Presto cluster using a cloud service.

Introducing Scalability

Operating Presto at scale means adding more resources to the system to handle an increased workload. The concept of scalability is slightly different from that of performance tuning, which you learned in Chapter 8. In fact, performance tuning is about making a system faster, while scaling is about handling more traffic.

Reasons to Scale Presto

If at least one of the following conditions occurs, it is appropriate to scale Presto: increase in the number of users, increase in the number of query requests, and increase in the volume of data (Figure 9-1).

To establish if it's time to scale your system, monitor your system's performance. You should scale your system when the performance drops due to more users, queries, or data load. Ideally, plan for this and do it before it becomes an issue.

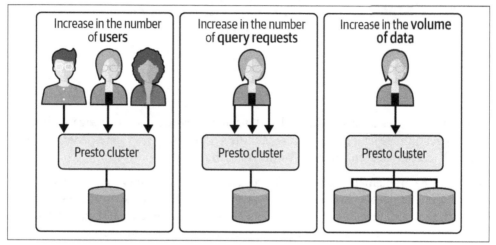

Figure 9-1. Some popular reasons to scale Presto

Common Issues

Before describing how to scale Presto, we'll explore some issues and limitations of a Presto cluster that needs to be scaled appropriately. The most common problems include single points of failure (SPOFs), a bad worker state, and bad queries.

Single point of failure

So far, you have deployed your Presto cluster using a single coordinator. The Presto coordinator maintains the Presto cluster's state and coordinates all node communication. It is also responsible for scheduling queries and managing query execution. The Presto coordinator is an SPOF because it is the only node in the Presto cluster that can perform certain functions. If the Presto coordinator fails, the entire cluster will be unavailable.

Bad worker state

Out-of-memory errors occur if a node tries to load more data into memory than its capacity. Such events can put the worker in a *bad state*. If a worker is in a bad state, any scheduled task for the same query fails. However, Presto continues the other tasks associated with the same query, thus wasting resources.

Bad query

A bad SQL query does not return the desired results or takes too long to execute. It can take over the compute resources and starve the other queries for resources. A SQL query may perform poorly due to the following reasons:

- *Inefficiency*: The SQL query is inefficient because it is not optimized to run as quickly as possible.
- *Overwhelm*: The SQL query uses more resources than the Presto cluster could handle.
- *Metastore overload*: There are too many SQL queries accessing the metastore for schema information.

Table 9-1 shows some popular types of queries causing inefficiency, overwhelm, and metastore overload.

Table 9-1. Some common bad queries

Inefficiency	Overwhelm	Metastore overload
Bad joins	Large tables with no partition/no partition pruning	A high query rate to `System.information_schema`
Inefficient comparison operators	Uneven partitions (skewed data)	
Missing partition filter	Too much data to load in Presto query engine	
Missing predicates		
Inefficient group/order by clauses		

Design Considerations

Design considerations for a large-scale Presto cluster must include several essential factors to ensure availability, manageability, performance, protection, and configuration.

Availability

There could be multiple occasions when a Presto cluster would require a restart, such as when you must upgrade the Presto version, or there is a JVM issue, such as a high garbage collection pause or out-of-memory error. In this case, while restarting, the cluster is unavailable. Availability measures how often a cluster is operational and available for use. To achieve high availability, you should design the cluster to tolerate the loss of any single node and continue operating without interruption.

A single Presto cluster may not satisfy the availability requirement, especially for some query types. Thus, you can use multiple Presto clusters serving different workloads simultaneously to guarantee high availability.

To manage multiple Presto clusters, you can use a *Presto Gateway*. A Presto Gateway is a policy-based query router for Presto clusters. For example, if one Presto cluster requires a restart, you can disable it at the gateway layer. When the same Presto cluster is healthy and ready to serve new queries, you can enable it again at the Presto Gateway. You can also automate this process by adding and removing Presto clusters based on load.

Consider the scenario described in Figure 9-2 to understand how the Presto Gateway works. There are two Presto clusters, 1 and 2, and one Presto Gateway. You can deploy the Presto Gateway by following the procedure described in its official documentation (*https://oreil.ly/nngVf*). Then, deploy two Presto clusters using different namespaces (`presto1` and `presto2`). Also, deploy the Presto coordinator services using two ports (`9001` and `9002`). To deploy the Presto clusters, use the code described in Chapter 5 or in Chapter 2 if your machine does not have enough resources to deploy two data lakehouses.

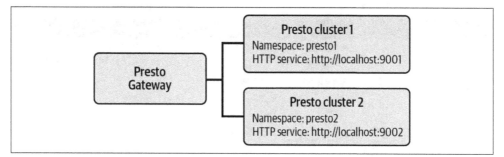

Figure 9-2. A scenario with two Presto clusters and one Presto Gateway

Once your system is running, the Presto Gateway listens for new connections at *http://localhost:8080*. Open a terminal and run the following command to add the two Presto clusters to the Presto Gateway:

```
curl -X POST http://localhost:8080/entity?entityType=GATEWAY_BACKEND \
  -d '{ "name": "presto1", \
        "proxyTo": "http://localhost:9001",\
        "active": true, \
        "routingGroup": "adhoc" \
     }'

curl -X POST http://localhost:8080/entity?entityType=GATEWAY_BACKEND \
  -d '{ "name": "presto2", \
        "proxyTo": "http://localhost:9002",\
        "active": true, \
        "routingGroup": "adhoc" \
     }'
```

Now both Presto clusters are active. For example, if you want to disable the Presto cluster `presto2` for some reason, run the following command:

```
curl -X POST http://localhost:8080/gateway/backend/deactivate/presto2
```

Recently, Presto has released the *Presto router*, a service sitting in front of Presto clusters. The Presto router is similar to the Presto Gateway. For more details on how to deploy it, follow the Presto official documentation (*https://oreil.ly/RTJ0Q*).

In this book, we chose to show how to manage multiple Presto clusters through the Presto Gateway because we wanted to demonstrate how you can easily integrate third-party code into Presto.

Manageability

Manageability specifies how efficiently and easily you can monitor and maintain your Presto cluster to keep the system performing, secure, and running. You have already learned how to administer your Presto cluster in Chapter 6. In addition to the already described concepts and strategies, Presto supports the event listener plug-in. You can implement the `EventListener` plug-in interface to intercept custom query events such as `queryCreated`, `queryCompleted`, and `splitCompleted`:

```
package com.facebook.presto.spi.eventlistener;

public interface EventListener {
  default void queryCreated(QueryCreatedEvent queryCreatedEvent) { }
  default void queryCompleted(QueryCompletedEvent queryCompletedEvent) { }
  default void splitCompleted(SplitCompletedEvent splitCompletedEvent) { }
}
```

Follow the Presto official documentation (*https://oreil.ly/uQ248*) and the AWS blog article (*https://oreil.ly/FN3Je*) to implement a custom event listener. Alternatively, use the sample event listener at the *aws-samples* repository (*https://oreil.ly/1Af-U*). Once you have built the event listener JAR file, copy it to the *plugin* directory of your Presto coordinator. Then, configure the event listener by adding the following *event-listener.properties* file to the *etc* directory of your Presto coordinator:

```
event-listener.name=event-listener
```

Restart your Presto cluster, log in to a Presto client, and run a simple query:

```
SELECT * FROM tpch.tiny.customer LIMIT 10;
```

Then, access the *log/queries-YYYY-MM-DDTHH\:MM\:SS.0.log* file in your Presto coordinator to see the output of the event listener plug-in.

You can use the query log files produced by the event listener to understand the overall health and performance of your Presto cluster. For example, the `QueryCompleted` event provides the failure type (user error or server error) along with the stack trace of the exception caught when the query failed. In addition, you can use query logs to check if queries have table partition filters present, if they involve a join, how much raw data each query is scanning, etc.

Performance

In Chapter 8 you learned how to tune the performance of a Presto cluster. From a design perspective, tuning the performance of Presto requires setting up a production-like cluster to run the production-like load. In Chapter 6 you learned how to set up a verifier to test the behavior of a new Presto version in a separate Presto cluster. However, the Presto verifier alone does not provide the environment to test the performance of your Presto cluster. In this case, you can use a *Replayer* system, which simulates the behavior of your Presto cluster using a test cluster.

Consider the scenario described in Figure 9-3. In the production environment, the Event Listener logs the queries made by the Presto Clients and stores them in an Event DB, which stores the workload of the Presto cluster. In the test environment, the Replay Service accesses the Event DB and regenerates the production workload by creating some Replay Clients. The Replay Clients query the testing Presto Cluster, and the test Event Listener logs the queries produced by the test Presto Cluster. Finally, the Replay Analytics and Reporting Service uses the query logs of both environments for debugging and performance improvement.

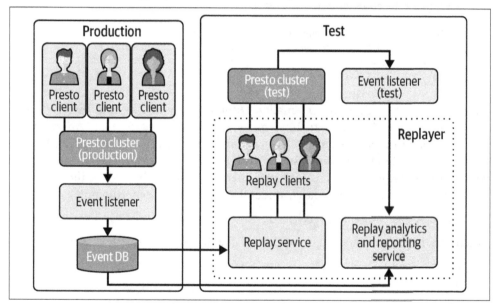

Figure 9-3. Setting up a test cluster using a Replayer

Protection

Because Presto is a distributed system, it is susceptible to bad actors who could potentially use it to launch attacks on the underlying infrastructure. In Chapter 7 you learned how to secure a Presto cluster and protect it from such threats. In addition, you can protect your Presto cluster from the injection of bad queries, thus preserving the cluster's resources. You can use the Presto Gateway to block or rewrite certain SQL queries.

Besides the Presto Gateway, you can implement query blocking using the event listener plug-in. Modify the `queryCreated` method to block some types of queries. For example, use the following code to block queries going to the table `system.information_schema.columns` that do not have any predicates (`where` clause):

```
public void queryCreated(QueryCreatedEvent queryCreatedEvent) {
    String queryText =
    queryCreatedEvent.getMetadata().getQuery().toLowerCase();

    if (queryText.contains("system.information_schema.columns") &&
        !queryText.contains("where")) {
      logger.error("Rejected query from event listener: " + queryText);
      throw new PrestoException(StandardErrorCode.COMPILER_ERROR,
            "Querying without predicates is not permitted.");
    }
}
```

Configuration

In Chapter 6 you learned how to configure a Presto cluster using properties, sessions, and JVM parameters. However, in a large-scale environment, this type of configuration alone may not be enough. You must also select the node type for the Presto coordinator and workers based on the cluster workload.

Selecting the right node type for the coordinator and workers is tricky as it depends a lot on the type of queries run on the system. You should define a long-term strategy for choosing the right mix of memory and CPU. To do this, you should collect JVM metrics. Ideally, during peak usage, the Presto coordinator should have 50% to 70% CPU and memory usage, and the workers should have 90% or higher CPU usage and 70% or higher memory usage. If either CPU or memory usage metrics are too high or too low, then the node type is not balanced in terms of resources.

Configure the *jvm.config* file with the following options in production:

`-server`
Selects the "server" VM. It is intended for running long-running server applications and is the default VM for server-class machines.

`-Djdk.attach.allowAttachSelf=true`
Allows the JVM to attach to itself for debugging purposes.

`-Xlog:gc:<path/to/log/dir>/gc.log`
Enables logging of garbage collection events to a file named *gc.log* in the directory specified by <path/to/log/dir>.

`-XX:+UseG1GC`
Enables the use of the G1 garbage collector.

`-XX:+AggressiveOpts`
Enables a set of aggressive optimizations that can improve performance.

`-XX:ReservedCodeCacheSize=150M`
Sets the size of the reserved code cache to 150 MB.

`-XX:ErrorFile={{ presto_log_dir }}/java_error.log`
Specifies the file to which error data should be written in case of a fatal error.

`-Xms{{ 0.80 * available_node_memory_mb }}m`
Sets the initial heap size to 80% of the available memory on the node.

`-Xmx{{ 0.80 * available_node_memory_mb }}m`
Sets the maximum heap size to 80% of the available memory on the node.

`-XX:MaxGCPauseMillis=400`
Sets a target for the maximum garbage collection pause time. The JVM will try to keep pauses shorter than this value.

`-XX:InitiatingHeapOccupancyPercent=5`
Sets a threshold for when the JVM should start a concurrent garbage collection cycle based on how much of the heap is occupied by live objects.

`XX:OnOutOfMemoryError="kill -9 %p"`
Specifies what command should be run when an `OutOfMemoryError` occurs. In this case, it will kill the process with ID %p.

`-XX:G1NewSizePercent=1`
Sets the initial size of the young generation (the part of the heap where new objects are allocated) to 1% of the heap size.

To enable JVM debugging, add the following options to allow a remote debugger to connect to the Java process:

```
-agentlib:jdwp=transport=dt_socket,server=y,suspend=n,address=5005
```

How to Scale Presto

To support a heavy workload, hours of runtime, and petabytes-size scans, you must scale the original Presto architecture. In this section, we will explore three approaches to scaling Presto: using multiple coordinators, running Presto on Spark, and spilling. These approaches are all designed to help organizations handle large data volumes efficiently and effectively.

Multiple Coordinators

Using multiple Presto coordinators enables you to scale your Presto cluster. The Presto coordinators control the life cycles of queries only, and a new component, called the *Resource Manager*, manages the cluster life cycle. A Presto cluster can have one or more Resource Managers, and Presto coordinators are independent of each other. Figure 9-4 shows a cluster with multiple Presto coordinators and Resource Managers. A new query is sent to an arbitrary coordinator, which sends it to the Resource Managers for queueing. Periodically, each coordinator fetches queries from the Resource Managers and decides whether to run it. The coordinators also poll the Resource Manager for information about active workers. For more details on how multiple coordinators work, read the "Disaggregated Coordinator" article (*https:// oreil.ly/-t0ig*).

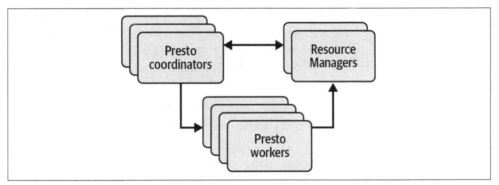

Figure 9-4. A Presto cluster with multiple coordinators

To configure multiple coordinators on your Presto cluster, add a new node for each Resource Manager. Use the following *config.properties* file for a cluster with a single Resource Manager:

```
resource-manager=true
resource-manager-enabled=true
coordinator=false
node-scheduler.include-coordinator=false
http-server.http.port=8080
thrift.server.port=8081
discovery-server.enabled=true
discovery.uri=http://<my_domain>:8080
thrift.server.ssl.enabled=true
```

The *config.properties* file disables the coordinator (coordinator=false) and enables the Resource Manager (resource-manager=true). Set the discovery.uri property to the URI of your Resource Manager.

Also, modify the *config.properties* file of your Presto coordinators and workers to include the following properties:

```
discovery.uri=http://<my_domain>:8080
resource-manager-enabled=true
```

The `discovery.uri` property must point to the Resource Group URI. Refer to the Presto documentation (*https://oreil.ly/L2Xzi*) for more details on configuring multiple coordinators.

Presto on Spark

Apache Spark (*https://oreil.ly/43UFX*) is an open source big data processing framework designed to be highly scalable and fault tolerant. You can deploy it on a standalone server or a cluster of hundreds of nodes. Since Spark runs on the JVM, you can easily integrate it with existing Java applications, including Presto.

There are many good reasons to run Presto on Spark. First, it can greatly improve the performance of Presto queries for very large batch ETL types, due to increased parallelism. Second, it can provide a more robust and scalable execution platform for Presto. Third, it can help to improve the stability and reliability of Presto deployments. Finally, it can enable Presto to take advantage of the many features and benefits of the Apache Spark ecosystem.

When you run Presto on Spark, you use only the Spark Resilient Distributed Dataset (RDD) level and below, without using the Spark SQL engine. RDD enables Spark to recheck data in case of a query failure.

Figure 9-5 shows the Presto on Spark architecture. The *Spark driver* runs a simplified version of the Presto coordinator, which parses and optimizes the queries and builds the query physical plans that are sent to the Presto workers installed on *Spark executors*. The Presto coordinator and workers are available as libraries, which only manage queries. Memory management, threading, and networking are instead delegated to the Spark cluster. For more details about the Presto on Spark architecture, refer to the "Scaling with Presto on Spark" article (*https://oreil.ly/UUpeT*).

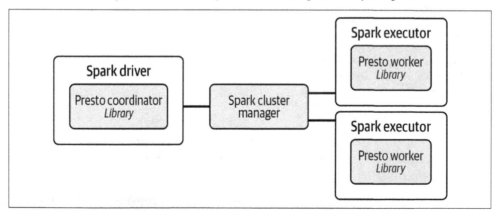

Figure 9-5. The Presto on Spark architecture

To run Presto on Spark, download the Presto Spark package and Presto Spark launcher JAR files from the Maven repository. Then, add the following properties to the Presto *config.properties* file:

```
task.concurrency=<N>
task.max-worker-threads=<N>
task.writer-count=<N>
```

The value of N must be consistent with your hardware. For most installations, a value of 8 or 16 is sufficient. Also, define your Presto catalogs as you usually do.

Then, define a query in a file named *query.sql*:

```
SELECT * FROM tpch.tiny.customer;
```

Finally, run the `spark-submit` command to invoke Spark, setting N to the same value as in the *config.properties* file:

```
/spark/bin/spark-submit \
--master spark://<url-to-spark-master>:7077 \
--executor-cores <N> \
--conf spark.task.cpus=<N> \
--class com.facebook.presto.spark.launcher.PrestoSparkLauncher \
  /path/to/presto-spark-launcher-0.280.jar \
--package /path/to/presto-spark-package-0.280.tar.gz \
--config /path/to/config.properties \
--catalogs /path/to/presto/catalog/directory \
--file query.sql
```

For more details on configuring Presto on Spark, follow the Presto official documentation (*https://oreil.ly/oHNzu*).

Spilling

In Chapter 6 you learned that spilling is moving memory to disk. Spilling allows Presto to continue processing queries even when it reaches memory limits. When a node runs out of available memory, it automatically writes some of the data to disk, freeing up space for additional processing. By spilling to disk, the cluster can handle larger queries and more concurrent users without running out of memory.

This scaling technique offers several benefits, including reliability improvement by reducing out-of-memory errors. It also reduces the risk of bottlenecks caused by overburdened nodes. Furthermore, spilling helps maximize hardware utilization and can reduce overall cluster costs by enabling the use of less expensive hardware. However, consider that spilling usually regresses performance significantly.

To enable spilling in Presto, set `experimental.spill-enabled` to `true`.

Using a Cloud Service

Implementing a Presto cluster from scratch can be a significant effort that requires expertise in distributed systems, networking, hardware configuration, and software setup.

Implementing a Presto cluster from scratch is:

Time-consuming
You should have time to set up nodes, install software, and configure network settings.

Costly
You should invest in hardware, software licenses, and ongoing maintenance and support costs.

Complex
You should have a high degree of technical expertise and knowledge.

Using a cloud service provider, like Amazon Web Services (AWS), Google Cloud Platform (GCP), or Microsoft Azure, can significantly simplify implementing a Presto cluster.

Cloud service providers help reduce the effort and cost of deploying a Presto cluster by providing preconfigured templates and automation scripts that simplify setup and management tasks. Additionally, cloud service providers offer features like auto-scaling, monitoring, and security tools that further simplify managing a Presto cluster.

Flexibility
Cloud services offer the flexibility to easily add or remove resources. This means that you can scale your Presto cluster up or down depending on the processing requirements of your queries without any up-front investment in infrastructure.

Cost savings
With cloud services, you pay only for the resources you use, making it a cost-effective solution for scaling up your Presto cluster. Additionally, you can reduce energy costs by running your Presto cluster on cloud instances optimized for workloads with high memory and CPU usage.

Reliability
Cloud services provide built-in redundancy and failover mechanisms that ensure your Presto cluster remains available even if a physical server fails.

Security
> Cloud services have advanced security measures, such as encryption and multifactor authentication, that help protect your data and prevent unauthorized access.

Scalability
> Cloud services are scalable, enabling you to add or remove nodes from your Presto cluster quickly and easily based on your changing processing needs.

Elasticity
> Cloud services offer the ability to automatically scale resources up or down based on demand, helping to optimize performance, utilization, and efficiency for your Presto cluster.

Conclusion

In this chapter, you learned how to scale a Presto cluster. Scalability measures how well a Presto cluster can handle increased workload or complexity without breaking down.

We discussed the basics of scalability and described some design considerations to achieve good scalability in a Presto cluster. We also explored popular approaches for scaling a Presto cluster, including multiple coordinators, Presto on Spark, and spilling. In the last part of the chapter, we described how to scale a Presto cluster using a cloud service.

You have just completed your journey in this book. Throughout this book, you have learned the basic concepts behind Presto, including its architecture, how to add data sources to Presto, and how to query them using different types of clients. Then, you have learned how to add Presto to a data lakehouse system using state-of-the-art technologies like Hive and Hudi. In the last part of the book, you learned how to administer, secure, tune the performance, and scale your Presto cluster.

Chapter after chapter, you have tested all the concepts learned through practical examples implemented ad hoc, which has allowed you to get your hands on the code and gain a practical understanding of how Presto works.

After reading this book, we hope that you will continue to learn more about Presto by reading other articles and books and actively participating in online communities dedicated to the topic.

Index

A

abstract syntax tree (AST), 133
access control, 77, 78
    authorization versus, 127
    configuring system access control, 126
    system, 38, 125
access-control.properties file, 126
ACID transactions, 74
ad hoc querying, 12
admin role, 125
administration of Presto, 91-113
    configurations, 92-98
        Java Virtual Machine, 96-98
        Presto configuration properties, 92-94
        sessions, 95-96
    introduction to, 91
    management, 104-113
        namespace functions, 110-113
        resource groups, 104-106
        session property managers, 110
        verifiers, 106-110
    monitoring a Presto cluster, 98-104
        metrics, 102-104
        using the console, 98-101
        using the REST API, 101
AI (artificial intelligence), 72
Altair library, 65
alternatives to Presto, 10
    Apache Hive, 11
    Apache Impala, 10
    Spark SQL, 11
    Trino, 11
Amazon Elastic MapReduce (EMR), 9
Amazon Simple Storage Service (S3), 73

Amazon Web Services (see AWS)
analysis (in performance tuning), 132
analytics
    advanced, in data lakehouse, 72
    open data lakehouse (see data lakehouse)
    real-time, with real-time databases, 13
ANSI SQL standard, 5
    Presto's compliance with, 7
Apache Hive (see Hive)
Apache Iceberg, 76
Apache Impala, 10
Apache Maven (see Maven)
Apache Pinot, 40, 51-55
    configuring Presto with Pinot, 53
    configuring to use with Presto, 52
    Presto-Pinot querying, 54
    setting up and configuring Presto for, 52
    setting up for connection to Presto, 52
Apache Ranger, authorization through, 127
    building custom audit function, 128
    integrating Presto and Ranger, 128
Apache Thrift (see Thrift)
apache-utils, 120
architecture and core components (Presto), 9
Aria scan, 139-140
    repartitioning, 140
    table scanning, 139
    testing, 146
ARM-based architecture, installing CentOS on, 19
artificial intelligence (AI), 72
AST (abstract syntax tree), 133
asymmetric encryption, 116
audit function (custom), 128

163

interactive plan (for queries), reviewing, 100
internal role, 125

J

Java
   Java 11 JRE, 96
   keystore file, presto-keystore.jks, 117
   presto-jdbc-0.276.jar file, 62
Java Development Kit (JDK), 42
Java Management Extensions (JMX)
   accessing metrics via REST API, 103
   exposing metrics via JMX exporters, 103
   JMX connector, 102
Java Virtual Machine (JVM)
   configuring, 96-98
      garbage collection, 97
      handling out-of-memory errors, 97
   configuring jvm.config in production, 155
   enabling debugging, 156
   jvm.config file, 21
JavaScript, Node.js client for Presto, 63
JDBC, 23
   client connectivity to Presto, 62
JDK (Java Development Kit), 42
JONI regular expression library, 94
JSON
   access control rules in, 126
   object returned from client query over
      REST API, 60
JsonCreator annotation, 47

K

Kerberos, 123-124
   configuring the Presto client, 124
   versus LDAP, 123
   prerequisites for, 123
keystore management, 117
keytab file, 123
keytool, 117
kubectl, 25
Kubernetes
   creating MySQL node that HMS will use to
      store data, 84
   creating pod for spark.yaml file, 86
   deploying Presto on, 25-32
      adding a new catalog, 31
      configuring Presto, 26-31
      introduction to Kubernetes, 25
      running the deployment, 32

node that runs Docker image in Presto clus-
    ter, 57, 58
Presto coordinator pod name, 141
querying Presto instance on, 32
wrapping Docker client-app Docker image
    in a node, 66
Kubernetes clusters
   creating HMS node in, 85
   data lakehouse components implemented as
      separate pods, 79
   deploying MinIO client as separate pod in
      the cluster, 82

L

LDAP (Lightweight Directory Access Protocol),
   122
   authentication based on, 119
   versus Kerberos, 123
LifeCycleManager object, 44
LINE_SPLITTER object, 51
LoadBalancer object, 66
log.properties setting, 23
logging
   enabling for garbage collection, 97
   log level in table formats, 75
   output of event listener plug-in, 153
LOG_VERBOSITY session property, 46

M

machine learning (ML), 72
manageability, 153
management of Presto, 104-113
   namespace functions, 110-113
      configuring a function, 112
      running a test, 113
      setting up the system, 111
   resource groups, 104-106
      configuring resource groups, 104
      example of use, 105
      resource group properties, 104
   session property managers, 110
   verifiers, 106-110
      configuring the MySQL database, 108
      configuring the Presto verifier, 108
      running a test, 109
      setting up the system, 107
MapReduce, 5
Maven, 42

RESET SESSION command, 95
Resilient Distributed Dataset (RDD) in Spark, 158
resource allocation, 136
    increasing, methods of, 136
    resources to increase depending on query type, 136
resource groups, 94
    configuring, 104
        resource group properties, 104
    example, 105
    URI, 158
Resource Managers, 157
REST API
    accessing JMX metrics via, 103
    authorizing access to, 125
    client query over, endpoints provided, 60
    using to monitor Presto, 101
    using to run Presto client, 60
router (Presto), 153

S
S3 (Simple Storage Service), 73
SAN (Subject Alternative Name), 117
sandbox (Presto), 24, 88
Scala, use in Spark shell, 87
scalability
    about, 149
    high scalability with Presto, 7
    introduction to, 149-151
        common issues, 150
        reasons to scale Presto, 150
    issues with data warehouses, 3
scaling
    how to scale Presto, 156-160
        Presto on Spark, 158
        spilling, 159
        using multiple coordinators, 157
    scaling out or horizontal scaling, 136
    scaling up or vertical scaling, 136
scheduler, 9, 39
    node scheduler configuration properties, 93
schema evolution, 74
schemas, 23, 47
    listing in query of Presto instance on Kubernetes, 33
    math schema, 112
    specifying for client query on REST API, 60
    specifying schema for JDBC client query, 63

table in Presto instance on Kubernetes, 35
tiny schema from TPC-H catalog, 67, 134
secrets, 28
    generating for MySQL server, 32
    MinIO, storing in Kubernetes cluster, 81
    presto-mysql-secrets, 111
    presto-secrets.yaml file, 31
security in Presto, 115-129
    authentication, 119-125
        creating custom authenticator, 124
        file-based, 120-122
        Kerberos, 123-124
        LDAP, 122
    authorization, 125-129
        authorizing access to REST API, 125
        configuring system access control, 126
        using Apache Ranger, 127
    building secure communication, 116-119
        configuring HTTPS/TLS, 118
        keystore management, 117
    encryption, 116
    introduction to, 115
    protecting your cluster from threats, 154
select command, 35
self-signed certificates, 117
    passing to Presto client, 119
semantic definition, 77
semi-structured data, 1
server module (Pinot), 52
Service Provider Interface (SPI), 37-38
session properties, 46
session property managers, 110
    configuring, 110
sessions
    configuring, 95
        changing value of session property, 95
    using, 95
SET SESSION command, 95
sf1 schema in Presto, 141
single point of failure (SPOF), 150
socket timeout exception, 33
Spark
    configuring for data lakehouse, 86
    converting CSV table format to ORC, 142
    converting CSV table to Hudi table, 87
    running Presto on, 158
Spark Docker image, creating for HMS in data lakehouse, 85
Spark SQL, 11

generating with htpasswd, 120
for MinIO, 81, 82

V

value-based parameters, 142
verifiers, 106-110
  architecture of system using Presto verifier, 107
  configuring, 108
  configuring the MySQL database, 108
  running a test, 109
  setting up the system, 107
vertical scaling, 136
volumes
  adding mount point and volume for JMX connector, 102
  mounting
    on Kubernetes, 28
    running custom script in Docker container, 59

warnings about, 59

W

web application
  client dashboard in Python, 66
  permitting access over HTTP, 58
web interface
  for MinIO, 82, 83
  Presto console, 98
workers
  bad worker state, 150
  configuring for Presto on Kubernetes, 29
  modifying config.properties to enable Kerberos, 124
  storing configuration to pass to worker pods, 30

Z

zookeeper module (Pinot), 52

About the Authors

Angelica Lo Duca is a researcher with a PhD in computer science. She works in research and technology at the Institute of Informatics and Telematics of the Italian National Research Council. Her research areas include data engineering, data storytelling, data science, data journalism, and web applications. She has also worked with network security, semantic web, linked data, and blockchain. Additionally, she serves as a professor at the University of Pisa, where she teaches data journalism.

Tim Meehan has been fascinated by data problems for much of his career. He's been working on the Presto project since 2018. He's currently works at IBM and heads the Presto Technical Steering Committee. Before IBM, he worked at Meta, Bloomberg, Goldman Sachs, among others.

Vivek Bharathan is the cofounder and principal software engineer at Ahana, an IBM company. Previously, Vivek was a software engineer at Uber where he managed Presto clusters with more than 2,500 nodes, processing 35 PB of data per day, and worked on extending Presto to support Uber's interactive analytics needs. Prior to Uber, Vivek was an early member of the query-optimizer team at Vertica Systems and made several contributions to the core database engine and the Vertica ecosystem. Earlier in his career at the Laboratory for Artificial Intelligence Research, he developed emerging technologies in decision-support systems and reasoning systems. His Presto contributions include the pushdown of partial aggregations. Vivek holds a M.S. in computer science and engineering from The Ohio State University.

Ying Su is the performance architect at Ahana, an IBM company, where she works on building more efficient and better price-performant data lake services on Presto and Velox. She has worked for Microsoft SQLServer and Meta Presto in the past and is a Presto committer and TSC board member.

Colophon

The animal on the cover of *Learning and Operating Presto* is a Greater Martinique skink (*Mabuya mabouya*). Not much is known about them. This lizard is endemic to Martinique, terrestrial in nature, and has bronze-colored skin with lighter strips on its upper flank.

There are over 1,500 known species of skink. Skinks are distinguished by having smaller legs in proportion to their body than most lizards, which makes their style of movement more similar to a snake. They are able to shed their tail if predators seize on that appendage, and can regrow it (at least partially) within a few months. Generally, skinks consume a diet of various insects, such as crickets, beetles, caterpillars, and flies.

The Greater Martinique skink is listed as critically endangered, and may possibly be extinct due to nonnative predators introduced on Caribbean islands. Many of the animals on O'Reilly covers are endangered; all of them are important to the world.

The cover illustration is by Karen Montgomery, based on an antique engraving from *Pictorial Museum of Animated Nature*. The cover fonts are Gilroy Semibold and Guardian Sans. The text font is Adobe Minion Pro; the heading font is Adobe Myriad Condensed; and the code font is Dalton Maag's Ubuntu Mono.

Printed in the USA
CPSIA information can be obtained
at www.ICGtesting.com
JSHW060012230923
49011JS00005B/10